CW00523535

WEMBLEY WIZARDS

WEMBLEY

WIZARDS

THE STORY OF A LEGEND

PAUL JOANNOU

MAINSTREAM
PUBLISHING

Copyright © Paul Joannou, 1990

All rights reserved

First published in Great Britain 1990 by
MAINSTREAM PUBLISHING COMPANY
(EDINBURGH) LTD
7 Albany Street
Edinburgh EH1 3UG

No part of this book may be reproduced or transmitted in any
form or by any means, mechanical or electric, including
photocopy, recording or any information storage and retrieval
system now known or to be invented, without permission in
writing from the publisher, except by a reviewer who wishes
to quote brief passages in connection with a review written for
a magazine, newspaper or broadcast.

British Library Cataloguing in Publication Data
Joannou, Paul
    Wembley Wizards.
    1. Association football. Scottish teams, history
    I. Title
    796.33466

    ISBN 1 85158 320 3

Typeset in 11/13 Baskerville by Bookworm Typesetting Ltd, Edinburgh
Printed in Great Britain by Martin's of Berwick, Berwick-Upon-Tweed

CONTENTS

INTRODUCTION

THE STORY OF A LEGEND

I FIRST EXPERIENCED a Scotland versus England confrontation as a teenager packed into the gravel embankment of Hampden Park in 1970, one of a 137,438 crowd. Few of that massive gate wanted an English victory; I hardly saw a Sassenach, at least anyone sporting the colours of the south. The passion of the Scottish fans was astonishing, their patriotism at times overwhelming.

Football occasions come and go and new competitions spring up but the traditional meeting of Scotland and England, the oldest international in the world, remains an exhilarating fixture. For decades only one match mattered, the annual do-or-die battle. It was the game players wanted to play in first. As Alan Morton noted, "The zest and enthusiasm for the match with the Auld Enemy will always arouse the Scot to a special effort."

Despite recent criticism of the match by some as a meaningless contest no longer required in the modern game, fans still appear to want the challenge retained, albeit maybe in a different format. Over 63,000 were attracted to Hampden Park in 1989 and 70,480 saw the fixture at Wembley in 1988. England boss Bobby Robson once said, "To both countries it is everything. Each badly wants to beat the other," while Graeme Souness, as Scotland captain, noted, "Beating England always leaves you with a lovely warm glow."

Of all the matches played in the 120-year history of the contest, one occasion is remembered and recollected more than any other. The last day of March 1928 was a rain sodden day, yet a day when 11 Scots crushed the English as they have never done since. The Blues, as *The Scotsman*'s observer noted, gave, "an irresistible display of dribbling, passing and shooting". They won 5-1, but it should have been six or seven. Never has Scotland given their great rivals such a football lesson as that afternoon in 1928. It was the day the "Wembley Wizards" were born . . . a title which still has a magical ring to it more than 60 years later.

This is a book about that victory, one of football's most famous moments. The story of the pre-match build-up, the debate, with profiles of each Scottish hero as well as their opponents, and of course detail of the action on the field.

1928 was a year when The Flying Scotsman started its non-stop service from Edinburgh to London and when the first £1 note came into circulation. As thousands of Scots headed towards the Empire Stadium at Wembley, headlines included events topical even today. In

Linlithgow, when canvassing for a by-election, Manny Shinwell and Lady Astor argued the values of socialism and disarmament, while the House of Commons heard a plea for Home Rule for Scotland with a separate assembly in Edinburgh. Even gang warfare erupted in Lanark as a bunch of hooligans known as the "Lazy O's" caused havoc.

Not only does this story spotlight Scotland's victory and the 11 stars, including several "All Time Greats" of the game, it also gives an insight to football during the years between the two wars: a Golden Age, when the country's top players received £8 per week, when Scotland's team came from 11 different clubs, when there was little or no coaching, no pre-match tactics and admission was all of one shilling.

Those 11 stars who earned immortality each had a fascinating career in the game. Many were colourful personalities who in this age would be megastars. Goalkeeper Jack Harkness embarked on a 50-year stay in football being twice capped when an amateur still in his 'teens. Full-backs Jimmy Nelson and Tommy Law both hailed from the banks of the Clyde like most of the side, but both found fame in the south. Jimmy Gibson came from a noted Lanarkshire footballing family and, after starring for Partick Thistle, became a member of Aston Villa's record goalscoring side. Partnering Gibson in the half-back line was Tom Bradshaw, big and broad yet possessing delicate skills, but after snuffing out the considerable threat of Dixie Dean, he never pulled on Scotland's shirt again. At left-half, Jimmy McMullan was skipper of the team, a commanding and respected professional despite his diminutive build. He had a career packed with incident.

Scotland's forward line was a dazzling yet often controversial collection of talent, containing five special characters. Alec Jackson and Alan Morton had no rivals on the flanks – they were a blend of flamboyant and subdued styles. In their own very different ways both created headline after headline. Hibernian playmaker Jimmy Dunn was at inside-right. He was to join an Everton team that won a treble of honours. Next to him was Alex James with his baggy shorts, then at Preston North End, who was to become the architect of Arsenal's Thirties' mastery. At centre-forward was Hughie Gallacher, school-chum of James, who caused more sensation than any other player of the era. Four of the five hardly topped five feet five inches in height . . . Scotland's smallest ever strikeforce, yet they mesmerised England's defenders.

They were 11 players whose careers spanned across many football tales and covered the exploits of the great sides like Rangers, Arsenal and Huddersfield Town as well as some of the more romantic stories with the rise to glory of the likes of Cardiff City, Partick Thistle and

Bury. There were many controversial moments, such as Alec Jackson's bold lone crusade over money, and some lighter incidents when Jimmy Dunn and Dixie Dean literally battled out a few rounds with German police.

This may be a book for traditionalists but the Wembley Wizards' story is now part of football's heritage. It has become folklore in Scotland. It was, too, a victory which set the pattern of the Scottish fans' much-enjoyed trek to Wembley, a stadium with a mystical attraction for both players and spectators. The Scots were henceforth to journey in their thousands and transform the English capital into a mass of tartan.

The Wembley Wizards were a special combination of football skills. They had never played together as a team before and, quite incredibly, were never to play together again.

Paul Joannou
Edinburgh
May 1990

ACKNOWLEDGMENTS

SEVERAL PEOPLE are to be thanked in the research of the story of that remarkable day in March 1928. Gratitude should be expressed to the Scottish Football Association and to past secretary Ernie Walker for permission to use the Association's archives which were invaluable.

The National Library of Scotland in Edinburgh was an invaluable point of reference and also a source of illustrative material. Bob Miller at the *Sunday Post* in Glasgow was of tremendous assistance in relating the career of Jack Harkness, a former media colleague.

While it has sometimes been infuriating trying to trace Scottish League and Cup statistics for the inter-war period, and for that matter FA Cup details south of the border, the following people have been of great help in piecing together the careers of Scotland's men at Wembley:
R. McElroy (Glasgow), S. Cheshire (Stoke), J. Maddocks (Manchester City FC), W. Laidlaw (Edinburgh), D. Lamming (N. Ferriby), P. Tully (Newcastle), J. Litster (Kirkcaldy), W. Hume (Dumfries), G. Blackwood (Edinburgh), B. Mark (Tranent), A. Cunningham (Edinburgh), H. Cooke (Glasgow), A. Ward (Oxford), G. Campbell (Ontario), K. Slater (Newcastle Utd FC), B. Horsnell (Reading), A. Rippon (Derby), A.F. Jones (Dumbarton).

Photograph Acknowledgments
Scottish Football Association, National Library of Scotland, G. Blackwood, D. Lamming, *The Footballer*, P. Joannou collection, A. Rippon, H. Gallacher Jnr.

The front-cover team group of the Wembley Wizards has been drawn by Canning Brothers Studios. As far as can be ascertained no photograph of Scotland's most famous line-up is in existence.

FOREWORD

BY ROY AITKEN, CAPTAIN OF SCOTLAND

IN MY GAMES for Scotland over the last decade I've only once been part of a side that has defeated England, and never at Wembley, to my great disappointment. Like every Scot, I fervently want to beat the Auld Enemy. It's a game all Scottish players want to play in and I've never known a single Scot who does not have that special feeling when the English are in opposition. We all get keyed up in the dressing-room before the game . . . the adrenalin runs fast. Bobby Lennox always said to me that the pleasure after toppling England, then World Champions, at Wembley in 1967 was unique. It was a day I remember as a youngster. The punters went crazy.

The atmosphere that surrounds the game is a one-off, whether at Hampden Park or Wembley, where Scottish fans continue to amaze me with their massive support. The Wembley Weekend is very much a way of life for Scotland's supporters. Having lived among them most of my life I know how much they look forward to a couple of days in London. It is a time for a very proud nation to show off and have a bit of fun.

The game of football needs tradition and nostalgia, like the "Wembley Wizards". Legends and hero figures are at the very heart of the sport. The game wouldn't be the same without these tales from the past, whether about Scotland's 1928 side or about latter-day events like Celtic's European triumph of 1967, or for that matter our recent double victory in Celtic's centenary year. In 50 years' time, the legend of that achievement will be nostalgia too.

I positively believe that the Scotland versus England meeting is still a match to be regarded as a spectacle. Having the game at the end of a long season is sometimes difficult for the players, coming on top of such a glut of fixtures, and perhaps a showpiece at the start of a season would be much better for all. It would be a sin to just end the battle after over a century of meetings. The satisfaction of putting one over the Auld Enemy is far too good for that!

"All Scotland should have been there to see it. Never has the Scottish style of football been more gloriously confirmed. Never has sheer ball-skill and artistry gained a greater triumph."

Ivan Sharpe, *Athletic News*, March 1928.

1

THE OLDEST INTERNATIONAL IN THE WORLD

The Scotland-England fixture provides an atmosphere which cannot be compared anywhere else.

Jock Stein

SCOTLAND VERSUS ENGLAND. A confrontation that stirs emotions in even the most placid of Scot. A meeting of nations that means far more than a simple game of football, especially in Scotland where passions are raised to a frenzied patriotic level, where Scots elevate the clash to something nearer a religion than a mere soccer rivalry – all in order to show the Auld Enemy, the English, that Scotland is supreme.

The eternal hostility Scots have towards the English goes deep into history. To defeat England provides a degree of revenge for many events of long ago whose origins have little to do with the game of football. It is not uncommon to see banners adorned with 'Remember Bannockburn' or portraying modern sources of irritation, like 'Scots Oil' or 'No Poll Tax', which have made English society from many a Scot's point of view more opulent and powerful. It is on the football field and on the terraces of the Scotland versus England clash that this deep-rooted national feeling is shown more than anywhere else.

For decades the meeting was a measure of which side was best in football anywhere in the world. That was certainly believed to be the case up to 1950 when European football was just starting to develop and South American sides had rarely taken the field in Britain. It was the match players coveted playing in most. It was a challenge almost unique in the game. Nowhere else saw such a furious battle on an annual basis with packed stadiums on both sides of the Border. Over 149,000 saw the clash at Hampden Park in 1937 while crowds approaching 100,000 regularly congregated at Wembley. In its heyday it transcended anything that could be produced by any other confrontation of nations. The late Jock Stein once noted, "The Scotland-England fixture provides an atmosphere which cannot be compared anywhere else", while Ernie Walker, past Scottish Football Association secretary, commented in one editorial, "it is the envy of other football associations around the world".

The annual challenge is in fact the oldest international fixture in the world. It was at the suggestion of Charles W. Alcock, secretary of the English Football Association, that the intense rivalry of 100 years and more all started. Organised football had originated in the south, the FA being formed in 1863, and when in 1870 Alcock wrote to *The Sportsman*, a leading London newspaper, in 1870 noting the

Charles W. Alcock played a leading part in the affairs of the English Football Association for over 40 years and was the chief promoter of international football.

start of international football, Scotland had yet to form its own ruling body.

The English administrator announced that leading members of the English and Scottish game would play each other on 19 February 1870. As it happened frost caused the cancellation of what was to be a historic occasion, but the first Scotland versus England meeting was rescheduled a month later, on 5 March. However, it was far from being a true encounter, rather a London English XI against a London Scottish XI. Scotland's side was made up of players with Scots connections, however dubious. They were from public schools like Harrow, from the Old Etonians, Oxford University and staff of the Civil Service.

The match was held at Kennington Oval, now more at home with international cricket. *The Sportsman* noted that a good crowd turned up, "in the presence of an assemblage of spectators such has, in point of numbers, never been equalled". Scotland went 1-0 ahead through "a long and rather lucky kick" by Crawford of Harrow School, but the English equalised near the end when Baker scored after "a most brilliant run". A 1-1 draw was perhaps a fitting end to the inaugural meeting.

Another pseudo international took place in that year, in November, and England won 1-0, then two more the following year in 1871 and another in the early months of 1872, all at The Oval. Scotland failed to

13

Arthur Fitzgerald Kinnaird, later Lord Kinnaird, was capped for Scotland in the early Auld Enemy internationals although born in London. An imposing character, he later became President of the FA.

win any of the contests. However all five internationals were completely unrepresentative. Included in Scotland's line-up for those early games were men hardly Scottish-based, or even Scots-born. The likes of W.H. Gladstone, a member of Parliament and son of the then Prime Minister, A.F. Kinnaird, later Lord Kinnaird and the Football Association's President, were included. Kinnaird was in fact an Englishman, but a noted Scottish landowner. Philanthropist Quintin Hogg was another in Scotland's side, while some of the so-called Scots, including A.K. Smith and William Lindsay, later turned out for England against Scotland.

It was not until the closing months of 1872 that the first official international took place. Again Charles Alcock led the way. The Football Association recorded in their minutes: "In order to further the interests of the Association in Scotland it was decided during the current season that a team should be sent to Glasgow to represent England." The problem was finding an opposition.

Queen's Park Football Club was then at the forefront of Scottish football. Those were the days before either Rangers or Celtic had been formed and it was the Mount Florida side that took up the English challenge. Queen's captain Robert Gardner picked the Scotland team to meet England. They were all either Queen's Park players, or ex-members of the club. Even the referee, William Keay, was from the Spiders' ranks.

Queen's Park 1873/74, featuring several pioneers of the Scotland v England meeting. Back row, left to right: McKinnon (A.), Dickson, Lawrie, Campbell, Neill. Front row: Leckie, Taylor, McNeil, Thomson, Weir, McKinnon (W.). Messrs Leckie, Taylor, Thomson, Weir and William McKinnon all appeared in the 1872 international with England. Angus McKinnon, McNeil, Campbell and Neill also played for Scotland in later years.

The game took place on St Andrew's Day, 30 November 1872, at the West of Scotland cricket ground at Hamilton Crescent in Partick which was the largest enclosure of the day in Scotland.

Football was a crude contortion of the modern game back in 1872. Rules featured both the new association code and traditional rugby laws and the scoring system relied to a degree both on goals and the odd touchdown. The announcement of the fixture caused considerable ill feeling from rugby enthusiasts who held the association code with distaste.

The sides' colours were as they are today . . . or almost. Scotland played in dark-blue jerseys boasting the rampant lion on the chest, white shorts, blue and white stockings and headgear of red cowls. England dressed in white shirts with the arms of England as a badge, dark-blue caps and white knickerbockers. Tactics were almost comic by present standards. Apart from goalkeepers who then could not, according to the rules, use their hands, the Scots operated with two full-backs, two half-backs and six

15

forwards. England on the other hand only had one back, one half-back and no fewer than eight men up front.

Despite the number of players around the two goalmouths the pioneers of international football could not manage a single goal and the first officially recognised Auld Enemy meeting ended in a 0-0 draw. Just over 4,000 spectators turned up on that grey, wet Saturday. They were the first of millions who in future years would become enthralled by the Scotland v England experience. The admission was one shilling and gate receipts totalled £102.19s.6d. *Bell's Life* described the occasion as "one of the jolliest, one of the most spirited and most pleasant matches that have ever been played". The *North British Daily Mail's* correspondent wrote: "For the first time this match was a real international, all the players of both teams being bona fide players in each country", while the *Glasgow Herald* noted, "the match was very evenly and toughly contested".

Future Scottish international full-back Wattie Arnott left a lovely anecdote of his experience of the match as a young lad. In the valued early football text, *Association Football and the Men Who Made It*, Arnott wrote: "Several of us determined to go and see it. When the Saturday came we started off in the forenoon to walk to the ground – a distance of nearly five miles; but after reaching our destination, found that there was no chance of getting inside the ground unless we paid at the gate. What few coppers we had among us were gone by this time." The young Glaswegians improvised though: "Just when we had given up all hope, we earnestly begged a cabman to accommodate us on the top of his cab and it was from that perch that I witnessed the first encounter between the two nations."

There was a dinner for the two squads at Carrick's Royal Hotel in the evening and arrangements were made for a return fixture the following year in London. The Scotland versus England series had kicked off.

The match gave a stimulus to the game in Scotland. The Scottish Football Association was formed soon after, in 1873. Scotland's first victory was a year later and they were the first winners of the Home International Championship a decade on. The Scots showed early dominance. From 1879 to 1888 the Dark Blues went nine years without defeat in any international. They had beaten England 6-1 at Kennington Oval in 1881 and 5-1 the following year. England had one or two good victories as well, notably 5-0 at Hampden in 1888 to end the home country's fine sequence. They also won 4-1 in 1892 at Ibrox, four goals coming in the first 21 minutes. But in the matches up to the turn of the century Scotland had only lost nine of the 29 meetings.

The Edwardian era was more evenly matched, while in the decade after World War One Scotland were again in the ascendancy, reaching a peak in performance. They won six of the meetings and lost only two. Venues

The Home International Championship trophy, first competed for in 1883/84 and won by Scotland.

started to switch on a regular basis to Hampden Park and to England's new national arena. Thus an important ingredient was added to the clash, one that generation after generation of Scots flocked to . . . the attraction of the Empire Stadium, Wembley.

2

WEMBLEY BOUND

We're on our knees and we know it . . . We have not native players who can be expected to hold their own with England's Association team at Wembley next month.
The Bulletin, March 1928

THE 1920s WAS a period of marked contrast in Britain. The First World War brought tragic loss of life, but in its aftermath sweeping and almost revolutionary alterations to society took hold of the population's lifestyle. The Roaring Twenties of the jazz phenomenon, the tango, wild parties and the sophisticated comedies of Noel Coward had shocked a pre-war establishment brought up on Victorian ideals. Much had changed since the days of 1914. People were now becoming prosperous and starting to obtain luxuries like cars, previously very much restricted to the gentry. Even the middle-class could now afford a Morris Oxford or Austin Seven at £170 – £25 down and £2 per week. But after economic boom a dramatic slump followed, creating high unemployment which quickly rolled into the Great Depression by the end of the decade . . . the Wall Street crash and all.

At first, though, life was good. George V was on the throne, the first monarch of the House of Windsor. A Labour Government was lodged in Downing Street for the very first time under Ramsay MacDonald while the death of Lenin at Gorki was announced in the same year. It was a decade that saw penicillin and television invented and women given full voting parity, and which welcomed the first solo flight across the Atlantic.

A generation that had had to live through the hostilities of Europe wanted entertainment and enjoyment. Silent cinema and Valentino were at their peak, with talkies quickly on the way. Al Jolson and Mickey Mouse were among the stars to make their débuts. Live theatre and music-hall comedy thrived while public houses experienced an exceptional trade. In one year the nation's drink bill was some £300 million. Slim young things danced the fast-moving Charleston and fashions saw women's hair boyishly short and skirts barely to the knee.

People idolised the famous, and sport provided plenty of personalities. Jack Dempsey was Heavyweight Champion in boxing, soon to be succeeded by Gene Tunney. Barota and Lacoste dominated tennis and Joe Davis did the same in snooker. The USA's golfers held a monopoly on the greens and Yorkshire and Lancashire vied for supremacy in cricket. On the soccer field it was boom time. Crowds paid their shilling a time and packed into every stadium with tremendous enthusiasm. Rangers

Willie McStay, Celtic's noted full-back.
He was one of the Scottish League side
to suffer against the English.

Goalscoring legend, Jimmy McGrory.
A fierce debate raged over his omission
from Scotland's line-up in favour of
Hughie Gallacher.

dominated the Scottish game while Huddersfield Town were the force in the south. Clubs now long gone like Arthurlie, St Bernard's, South Shields and Merthyr Town were included in League fixture lists.

A galaxy of stars graced the field and the masses had heroes galore – names like Charlie Buchan, Patsy Gallacher, Andy Wilson and Jimmy Seed. As the decade kicked off, footballers earned £8 per week plus bonuses of £2 for a win and £1 for a draw. They could pick up an extra £6 if they played in an international. They wore baggy shorts, thick, flapping jerseys and clumsy-looking boots. They kicked a heavy laced ball and rarely were embroiled in tactics or training as we know them today. A few sprints round the pitch and a long brisk walk was the normal daily exercise.

Even when the economic depression swept over the country it did not dampen people's craving for soccer. A general strike occurred in the Spring of 1926 and by the end of the Twenties almost two million were unemployed, yet football, the people's sport, remained the main outlet from increasing despair.

In 1928 the Ibrox men were on their way to the double in Scotland, while Everton's Dixie Dean was creating havoc on English grounds, banging home a total of 82 goals in all games in the season. David Jack had moved from Bolton Wanderers to Arsenal for a record £10,890 fee, the first transfer to break the five-figure barrier.

The Twenties were halcyon days for football and for Scottish international soccer in particular. The Scots had an abundance of quality players in all positions. In 1920/21 they won all three Home International Championship games and carried off the trophy. It was the start of a decade of mastery. They played 34 internationals, won 24, only lost 5 and in a consecutive spell scored almost 20 goals without reply.

The Scots produced players with a flamboyant style and a liking for the big match atmosphere. They were a somewhat moody, temperamental bunch but with the ability to produce the goods in feats of brilliant football, much as Scottish international football has continued since. Bob Crampsey has written that Scotland's teams "see-saw dizzily between heights and depths of attainment". The Twenties were years of heights and they reached their pinnacle at Wembley in March 1928.

The early games of the 1928 international calendar, however, were anything but masterly displays from Scotland. *The Bulletin*'s reporter was pressed to note Scotland's performances as "of a disastrous nature". Against Wales at Wrexham, the Scots were two goals in front inside the first quarter of the game but the Welsh fought back to equalise at 2-2. Changes were made for the next international: Celtic's Jimmy McGrory won his first cap. But at Firhill, Ireland went one better than Wales, winning 1-0. It was a frustrating afternoon for Scotland as Elisha Scott put on a tremendous display of goalkeeping for the Irish.

There was much debate as to why Scotland had failed so miserably and as to the team selection for the match that mattered above all, the Auld Enemy clash due on 31 March. Scottish selectors had two fixtures in which to assess candidates before the trip to London. On 10 March at Ibrox the Scottish League entertained the Football League in the prestigious annual challenge. It was a crucial test for several Scots players as the game, to all intents and purposes, was a Home Scots v England match. However the selectors were given an emphatic answer to the call from many quarters to field a predominantly Scottish based team in the forthcoming England and Scotland meeting: the Football League thrashed the Scots by 6-2 in front of a disillusioned 60,000 crowd. The home side contained six Rangers and Celtic men, including popular stars McStay, McGrory and Cunningham. Motherwell's exciting pair of Stevenson and Ferrier played, as did Lambie of Partick Thistle and Morton of Kilmarnock, all on the fringe of international selection. Celtic's goal-ace McGrory, much petitioned for the Scotland centre-forward shirt, grabbed two goals, but he didn't impress the selectors. Nobody, Hugh Morton excepted, played well and *The Bulletin* commented on Scotland's dismal failure in pessimistic tone: "We're on our knees and we know it, and for the first time in many years we will frankly admit that we have not at the moment native players who can be expected to hold their own with England's Association team at Wembley next month." The Scottish FA's representatives took note of the performance – or lack of it. None of the Home Scots was selected for the Wembley game while the Football League side contained eight players originally picked for the English combination.

Three days later at Firhill the final trial match took place. A selection of Home Scots faced Anglo-Scots on a bitterly cold evening, on a frost-bound pitch and with snow in the air. Only 6,000 saw the 1-1 draw but, importantly, several Anglos showed up well despite the conditions, notably Nelson, James, Bradshaw and Law. New faces were tried in the Home Scots' line-up but only one survived through to Wembley, Queen's Park goalkeeper Jack Harkness. All told, almost 40 players were on the selectors' short list and in with a chance of a Wembley trip. They were:

Goalkeepers Harkness (Queen's Park), Crawford (Blackburn Rovers), Robb (Rangers), McClory (Motherwell)

Defenders Gray (Rangers), McStay (Celtic), Nelson (Cardiff City), Law (Chelsea), Hutton (Blackburn Rovers)

Half-backs Meiklejohn (Rangers), Lambie (Partick Thistle), Craig (Rangers), Duncan (Leicester City), Bradshaw (Bury), McMullan (Manchester City), Gibson (Aston Villa), Morton (Kilmarnock), Macfarlane (Celtic), Muirhead (Rangers)

Inside-forwards Chalmers (Celtic), McPhail (Rangers), Lochhead (Leicester), James (Preston), Cunningham (Rangers), Dunn (Hibernian), Stevenson (Motherwell), McCrae (St Mirren), McKay (Newcastle United)

Centre-forwards McGrory (Celtic), Jennings (Leeds United), Gallacher (Newcastle United)

Wingers Gavigan (St Johnstone), McClean (Celtic), Jackson (Huddersfield Town), McLachlan (Cardiff City), Morton (Rangers), Ritchie (Hibernian)

Many didn't really have much hope of making the final side. When the selectors met at the Scottish Football Association's HQ in Carlton Place on 21 March, the nine-man committee led by the President, Robert Campbell of St Johnstone, took only 40 minutes to announce their party. They had undoubtedly agreed that several positions picked themselves. At first the waiting media gasped when the team was announced. It contained eight Anglos, only three home-based players, two men winning their first caps, another only his second, a centre-forward who had not kicked a ball in earnest for two months and a tiny front line that had little chance of winning the ball in the air. It read;

Goalkeeper Harkness (Queen's Park)
Full-backs Nelson (Cardiff City), Law (Chelsea)
Half-backs Gibson (Aston Villa), Bradshaw (Bury), McMullan (captain, Manchester City)
Inside-forwards Dunn (Hibernian), James (Preston)
Centre-forward Gallacher (Newcastle United)
Wingers Jackson (Huddersfield Town), Morton (Rangers)
Reserve Craig (Rangers)
Trainer Jimmy Kerr (Rangers)

Then, just as it would now, a huge outcry followed because of the number of Anglos in the side, although most judges with time to contemplate agreed with the selection. But initial reaction was expected when celebrated players from the Old Firm were dropped or overlooked. Scottish fans, especially the Glasgow-based ones, are fervently nationalistic, always wanting to see home stars in a Scotland shirt. To many the players who had flocked south, like Gallacher, James, Gibson and Jackson, were traitors to the cause, and, at times they were harshly treated, despite the fact that they had Scottish blood as good as any home-based player.

Out of the reckoning went the Rangers trio of Cunningham, McPhail and Davie Meiklejohn. Full-backs Willie McStay and Jock Hutton were axed, as was Jimmy McGrory, such a prolific goal-getter with 49 League goals in 1926/27 and 47 in 1927/28. The omission of McStay and Hutton, as *The Bulletin* noted, "was not unexpected" as Scotland were due to face two England wingers on top form, Hulme and Smith. The relatively inexperienced Anglos, Tommy Law and Jimmy Nelson, came in because of their knowledge of the English style of play.

The preference of Hughie Gallacher to McGrory caused a raging debate. Gallacher had up to then created an imposing set of statistics in a Scotland shirt – ten goals in only 11 games played. McGrory, for all his goals at club level, never threatened the ex-Airdrie and Newcastle leader for the centre-forward position. Even when Gallacher was out of football for several weeks prior to the England trip due to suspension, the selectors always had the fiery Bellshill lad ahead of Celtic's hero. Gallacher was to relate: "It was a great tribute to me – I was in disgrace and even more important had not played football for two months." The bustling McGrory never fitted Scotland's centre-forward profile. The press noted that, "there will always be a feeling that McGrory lacked the individual touches that one associates with an international centre-forward", and that, "Scotland certainly require a leader who can play football apart

Davie Meiklejohn and Bob McPhail, both of Rangers, two of several established Home Scots to be overlooked.

from specialising as a goalscorer". Gallacher fitted the bill perfectly, as did his predecessor Andy Wilson.

Both Tom Bradshaw of Bury and Tommy Law of Chelsea won their first caps for Scotland, while Preston's Alex James was to play in only his second international game. Additionally Jimmy Dunn, Jack Harkness, who was still an amateur, and Jimmy Nelson possessed only a handful of internationals behind them. It was a raw, inexperienced side. Reservations were noted, especially as to how unknowns Bradshaw and Law would cope against the power and swiftness of Dean and Hulme.

Questions were also asked about what was thought to be the smallest forward line ever to be fielded by a Scotland side. Alec Jackson, at five feet ten inches, was the only player who could be classed as tall. Dunn and James were five feet six inches, while both Morton and Gallacher were an inch shorter. *The Bulletin* commented: "The only fault that can be urged against the forwards is their lack of height." However Hughie Gallacher wrote, "skill and speed can make up for lack of inches", true words indeed, as it turned out. Alex James said, "Never before had a team been so severely panned by the critics. We were given no chance but we were never really discouraged." Gallacher added, "We were determined to show the critics that they could not have been more wrong."

Wembley Stadium. The main entrance area and twin towers under construction.

The completed ground ready for the British Empire Exhibition and FA Cup final.

An aerial view of Wembley, much as it looked in 1928 with vast open terraces.

Scotland's footballing history, before and after 1928, is littered with wee gems, tanner ba' players brought up on cobbled streets and not usually more than five feet seven at most. With Jimmy McMullan, another only five feet five, Scotland fielded five mighty midgets at Wembley. Others followed in the blue shirt of Scotland, names like Bremner, Johnstone, Henderson, Collins – a list that is almost endless. After Wembley in 1928 no one ever again doubted the ability of Scotland's short-legged terriers.

The Scottish press soon followed the early disagreement on the Scottish FA's choice with an almost unequivocal backing. *The Bulletin*'s own selection was almost fully correct, so they could not complain and noted, "In our opinion it is practically the best selection possible." But they added a pessimistic note and a warning on what might happen. In the south, *The Times* observed that Scotland's team looked "remarkably well balanced".

Scottish fans, though, had to be convinced. There was only one player, Alan Morton, from the Glasgow giants and several they had hardly heard of, never mind seen play week in week out. Yet, despite being inwardly concerned that another Ibrox scoreline might result, they, as ever, were extrovertly buoyant and optimistic. They looked forward to a weekend in England, in London, at its new national arena, the Empire Stadium.

LONDON MIDLAND AND SCOTTISH RAILWAY.

International Football Match
ENGLAND v. SCOTTLAND
At WEMBLEY

LMS

EXCURSIONS
TO
LONDON

by Special Corridor Trains on Friday night, 30th March, as under

From	By Train leaving at	Third Class Return Fares.
	p.m.	s. d.
GLASGOW (St Enoch)	10.30 & 11.0	25 6
EDINBURGH (Pr. St.)	8.50	24 0
DUNDEE (West)	8.50	27 0
ABERDEEN	6.10	28 6
ANNAN	10.38	22 6
AUCHINLECK	9.17	24 0
AYR	8.45	24 0
BLANTYRE	11.10	24 0
BRECHIN	6.10	27 0
BRIDGE OF ALLAN	9.34	25 6
CALLANDER	8.5	25 6
CAMBUSLANG	8.41	24 0
CARLUKE	k12.13a	24 0
CARSTAIRS	9.55p	24 0
CASTLE DOUGLAS	7.44	24 0
COATBRIDGE	8.3	24 0
COUPAR ANGUS	7.54	27 0
DALBEATTIE	7.54	22 6
DREGHORN	9.44	24 0
DUMFRIES	10.57	22 6
DUNBLANE	9.30	25 6
FALKIRK (Grahamston)	8.32	25 6
FORFAR	7.34	27 0
GLENEAGLES	9.49	25 6
GLENGARNOCK	9.15	25 6
GRANGEMOUTH	8.25	25 6
HAMILTON (Central)	11.21	24 0
HOLYTOWN	9.5	24 0
IRVINE	9.58	24 0
KILMARNOCK	9.25	24 0
KILWINNING	9.30	25 6
KIRKCONNEL	10.16	24 0
LANARK	8.7	24 0
LARBERT	10.33	25 6
LARKHALL (Central)	7.56	24 0
MAUCHLINE	9.7	24 0
MONTROSE	6.20	28 6
MOTHERWELL	11.42	24 0
NEW CUMNOCK	9.57	24 0
OLD CUMNOCK	9.24	25 6
PAISLEY (Gilmour St.)	8.50	25 6
PERTH	9.20	24 0
RUTHERGLEN	8.35	24 0
SANQUHAR	10.25	24 0
SPRINGSIDE	9.50	25 6
STIRLING	10.12	24 0
STONEHAVEN	6.56	28 6
WISHAW (Central)	11.59	24 0

k Early Morning of 31st March.

Handbills with full particulars of Return Train Times, etc., free at LMS Stations.

L·N·E·R

ENGLAND v. SCOTLAND
At Wembley
UNIVERSITY BOAT RACE
OXFORD v. CAMBRIDGE
Saturday, 31st March

On Friday night, 30th March
One Day Excursion
TO
LONDON
(King's Cross)

25/6 RETURN FARE THIRD CLASS **25/6**

Leaving GLASGOW (Queen St.) 7.50 p.m.
Cheap Period Excursion Tickets for 5, 6, or 8 days will also be issued by this train.

NOTE:—The Day Excursion tickets will be available for travel from London (Marylebone) to Wembley (Exhibition Station) and back on Saturday, 31st March. Tickets to the Exhibition Station (L.N.E.R.) will be available only by the L.N.E.R. Company's route from Marylebone to Wembley and do not include conveyance between King's Cross and Marylebone.

Non-stop trains will be run every few minutes from Marylebone to the Exhibition Station (adjoining Stadium), commencing at 1.10 p.m., the journey occupying 12 minutes.

Marylebone Station can be readily reached by electric train or motor 'bus.

Handbills with full particulars of return times, etc., free at L.N.E.R. Stations.

Tickets, bills, etc., can also be obtained from Moses Buchanan, 22 Renfield Street, and L.N.E.R. Town Office, 37 West George Street.

Scottish fans flocked to London in their thousands. Advertisements in the local press gave travel arrangements.

A group of the tartan army in London's West End before the game.

Wembley was barely five years old in 1928 and was just beginning to possess that irresistible aura that football fans, especially the Scots army of kilts, tammies, bagpipes and all, longed to be part of. On 8 May 1921 a Football Association committee, charged with the responsibility of finding a national stadium, had signed a 21-year agreement. The site was on the spot of a gigantic steel structure planned to rival the Eiffel Tower. It was a folly that never got beyond the first stage. Wembley was part of the Empire Exhibition, the biggest fair Britain had ever known, sprawling 216 acres over Wembley Park, then a small suburb of London with green fields, hills and a golf course – a virtually unknown dot on the Metropolitan Line to Harrow on the Hill. The Exhibition was a vast advertisement to a declining British Empire, but almost 30 million people swarmed to Wembley. They could visit such exhibits as a reconstruction of the tomb of Tutenkhamon and the most popular and enchanting Queen's Doll's House. There was a gigantic fun-fair, a huge market-place and side-shows whichever way visitors turned. There was even a statue of the Prince of Wales made from Canadian butter! It was inspiring yet laughable, but it brought football to Wembley, although it wasn't called that for some time. It was known simply and majestically as the Empire Stadium.

Early in 1922 the Duke of York, later King George VI, ceremoniously cut a piece of turf and within 12 months the ground took shape. Many contributors gave funds to build it including, ironically, the people of Glasgow who sent a collection of £105,000, as if they knew it would become something of a second home. Wembley was ready for the 1923 FA Cup final with only four days to spare. Its focal point was two grandiose twin towers of white stone which dominated the landscape for miles around. It had a capacity of 126,500 but maybe as many as 200,000 crammed through the gates, and over fences, for the West Ham v Bolton Wanderers Cup final and Wembley was immediately in the headlines ... white horse, Billie, and PC Storey on the front pages nationwide. From that remarkable beginning, Wembley – its exquisite green surface, its fascinating echo – possessed a special quality of its own unrivalled by any other ground.

The first visit by Scotland to the Empire Stadium was in 1924, a dull encounter that ended all square at one goal each. The 5,000 or so Scots who travelled to London in pioneer style brought back tales of the metropolis, the sights of Piccadilly Circus, Trafalgar Square, Parliament and the twin towers of Wembley itself. It was rare in those days for working-class Scots to venture far from their home town or city. A trip to Glasgow or Edinburgh was a treat, a journey to London, in many cases, a dream.

Scots fans relished their next weekend in London, although they had to wait four years, as the 1926 fixture was played at Old Trafford, Manchester. When the Spring of 1928 arrived and posters displaying travel arrangements went up, thousands were ready to flock over the Border. Many had saved hard over the previous months, a few shillings every week to pay for the trip which cost up to 28s.6d., third-class return. 1928 was the start of what was to be, for generations to follow, the traditional Wembley Weekend, when a taste of Scotland, full of colour, wit and mostly boisterous good humour, engulfed London. It was a brief escape from industrial homelands, especially from areas around Lanarkshire, Ayrshire and the Clyde. To many it was the only holiday of the year.

Elaborate arrangements had been made to cope with the migration, but even those were swamped by the numbers wanting to go. In days when road travel was in its infancy, there was only one way to go ... by train. Special excursions left from practically every town in Scotland. From St

THEY MIGHT HAVE MADE IT A FOURSOME!

ALAN MORTON (to Harkness and Dunn)—"If we'd only had another home Scot in the team we might have had a rubber of bridge." Only three home Scots travel south to take part in the international match at Wembley, the other eight players being Anglo-Scots.

The now famous cartoon which was published in The Bulletin *on 30 March 1928 as Scotland's depleted squad of home-based players headed south.*

Enoch's station in the heart of Glasgow trains left at ten thirty or 11 o'clock on Friday evening, and from Princes Street in Edinburgh at eight thirty.

Special groups were organised from clubs and works. There was even an ex-Scotland footballers' party. Bob McColl, the country's former centre-forward and then successful businessman, organised a reunion of surviving internationals from the Scotland team that faced England in

The Emergency & Finance Committee met in the Rooms 6 Carlton Place Glasgow on Wednesday 11th April 1928 & passed the undernoted statement in connection with International match v England at Wembley on 31st March 1928.

	£	s	d	£	s	d
J. D. Harkness	—	—	—			
J. Nelson	7	18	—			
T. Law	6	—	—			
J. Gibson	8	4	—			
T. Bradshaw	9	—	—			
Jn. McMullan	9	—	—			
A. Jackson	9	—	—			
J. Dunn	6	—	—			
H. Gallacher	10	—	—			
A. James	6	—	—			
A. Morton	6	—	—			
T. Craig	6	—	—			
J. Kerr	9	—	—	92	2	—
Commercial Union Assembly				10	—	—
Sundries				1	17	8
J. R. Charlton				4	8	6
T. Cook & Son				277	7	8
Gratuities etc paid by J. Graham				6	19	6
— — — Treasurer				23	9	=
J. Fleming				—	15	3
R. Buchanan				3	15	6
J. Jamison				—	1	4
				£206	6	8

Extract from the Scottish Football Association's original accounts book for 1928 detailing expenses for the trip to Wembley. Travel arrangements cost £277.7s.8d. while players received varied amounts. Gallacher earned £10, James £6, while Jack Harkness, the amateur in the side, didn't receive a penny.

1900. All 11 veterans, except the late Nicol Smith, travelled to Wembley sporting the colours of Lord Rosebery, the strip they wore at the turn of the century.

Almost 10,000 fans were on the move – perhaps not many by modern standards, but over 60 years ago it was a vast number. Eleven special trains left Glasgow alone, 33 altogether from the west of Scotland, and all converging on Carlisle at close intervals. To avoid congestion they were then split, some heading south via Leeds and others through Crewe.

A noisy tartan army moved towards London. In years to come it would grow larger and larger. It was a carnival occasion, even though they were cramped in old, uncomfortable carriages. That mattered little. With plenty of drink the fans sang, gambled and spoke of the forthcoming battle against the Auld Enemy. They discussed the players' strengths, their weaknesses, names that should have been playing and how Scotland would stop the Dixie Dean goal-machine. The steam trains headed south on their slow 12-hour journeys, arriving in the capital, at Euston, St Pancras and King's Cross, on Saturday morning. Many trooped on to the platform the worse for wear, tired, grubby and rolling drunk. But after they had a quick wash-up, shave and breakfast, the wail of the pipes could be heard all over London.

There was much colour and regalia as the Scots filed down Tottenham Court Road towards the West End – tartan scarves, tammies, kilts and sporrans, everything except the battle swords of Bannockburn. Some even proudly showed off the *sgian-dhu*, the traditional dagger in their stocking. It was all essentially light-hearted. There was plenty of alcohol but no fighting, no hooliganism, and Londoners welcomed their visitors.

Journalist Ian Woolridge wrote in the *Daily Mail* on a much later invasion of Scots, "Mostly they're five feet tall, unintelligible of tongue, have chips on their shoulders, bells on their hats, and carry an off-licence in both overcoat pockets." A somewhat cruel description but a characteristic English viewpoint. John Rafferty noted in the *Daily Express* on another modern visit, "They go charged with all the fervour of the raiding bands of old . . . they are going to the Mecca, the Everest, of football." On their way to Wembley and what was a gathering of the clans, exiled Scots in the south met up with their countrymen and transformed the terraces into a giant ceilidh, ablaze with tartan.

Many stopped off at the team's hotel *en route*. Unlike modern day football, when seclusion takes priority, Scotland's base was slap-bang in the middle of London's razzmatazz, the Regent's Palace Hotel in Piccadilly Circus, giving the impression that the players were also in London for a holiday weekend. Scotland's party had travelled on the Friday by the salubrious Royal Scot, in reserved carriages at a total

22. *International Match v. England.*

TIME-TABLE.

March 30	10.0 a.m.	Leave Central Station, Glasgow.
	12 0 noon	Lunch—Dining Car.
	4.0 p.m.	Afternoon Tea - Dining Car.
	6.15 ,,	Arrive Euston Station, London — Drive to Regent Palace Hotel.
	7 0 p.m.	Dinner.
March 31	9.0 a.m.	Breakfast. (Oxford & Cambridge Boat Race commences 9.30 a.m.)
	12.0 noon	Lunch.
	1.15 p.m.	Leave Hotel for Wembley.
	3.0 ,,	Kick-off.
	5 0 ,,	Return to Regent Palace Hotel.
	6.30 ,,	Dinner.
April 1	9.30 a.m.	Breakfast.
	11.15 ,,	Drive to Dorking.
	1.45 p.m.	Lunch Deepdene Hotel.
	4.30 ,,	Leave Dorking.
	7 0 ,,	Dinner—Regent Palace Hotel.
April 2	8.30 a.m.	Breakfast.
	9.20 ,,	Leave Hotel for Euston Station.
	10.0 ,,	Leave London.
	1.0 p.m.	Lunch.—Dining Car.
	4 30 ,,	Afternoon Tea—Dining Car.
	6.15 ,,	Arrive Central Station, Glasgow.

The Wizards' itinerary for the Wembley weekend as recorded in the Scottish FA's minutes of meeting for 1928.

cost of £277.7s.8d. In fact it was a depleted squad as only four players made the journey – Harkness, Morton, Dunn and reserve Tully Craig – the rest making their own arrangements from their respective English towns. There were not the elaborate preparations for the Wizards we would expect to see for international teams today – no League matches cancelled, no week-long get-together, no television or radio interviews.

Supporters eager to see their heroes spilled into the Regent's Palace foyer all Friday evening and Saturday morning. They milled together with the players in an atmosphere of jovial excitement. Tongues wagged and drink flowed. While the players kept their spirits up, some had reservations. Hughie Gallacher was to say, "A better spot would have been far in the country." Alex James was to note that a piper encamped outside the hotel all night playing his repertoire of tunes, "Nothing could stop him." It was hardly the best of preparations.

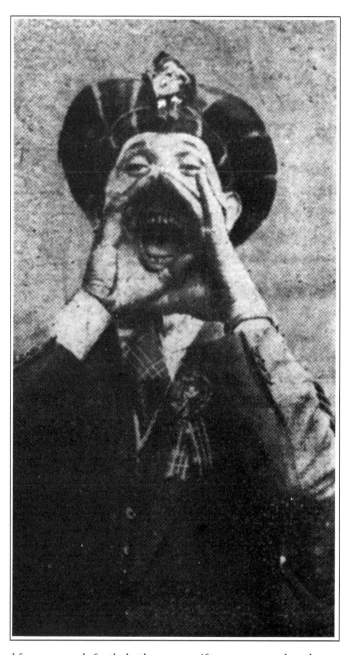

Scotland fans were ready for the battle . . . as vociferous as any modern-day supporters.

There had been much good-humoured rivalry between the players' camps. England's centre-forward Dixie Dean had left Jack Harkness a brown paper parcel at the hotel reception. When the Scotland 'keeper opened it he found a bottle of aspirins wrapped in a note which read, "Have a good sleep Jack. I'll be around tomorrow!"

Scotland's players watched the Oxford-Cambridge Boat Race before heading for Wembley on Saturday morning. Many Scots fans were there too, witnessing the traditional annual university challenge on the Thames. There was time for an audacious trip by Jackson and James to England's hotel to continue the banter between the sides. The Huddersfield winger aimed to needle his club team-mates in England's ranks, just as Dean had done to Harkness the night before. The two extrovert Scots bragged to their rivals that they would show how football should be played . . . the Scottish way. The Scots forwards also had a wager as to who would score first. James said to his colleague, "Bet you ten bob I score the first goal today." Jackson agreed but added, "And we'll make it a treble stake for a hat-trick."

After the pre-match relaxation it was off to Wembley for both players and fans. The Scotland team had a light lunch and at 1.15 p.m. a coach drive through the city. For the fans it was a dash to Baker Street and Marylebone for a train to the Exhibition Station.

Wembley had not seen anything quite like it. In the 1923 Cup final the numbers were vast and quite exceptional, but the colourful clan of Scots congregating around the twin towers was something totally different. Some even brought with them scaling ladders to make sure they saw the game. The bagpipes played again, the Scots sang out and the English looked on in astonishment at the pride and passion of Scottish support: 31 March 1928 was to be the day of the Wizards, a delirious day when Scottish football reached a peak.

J. NELSON J.D.HARKNESS T. LAW

SCOTLAND

J. GIBSON T. BRADSHAW J. M'MULLAN

A.JACKSON A. L. MORTON

J. DUNN H GALLACHER A.JAMES

3

JACK HARKNESS . . . JACK O' HEARTS

An agile 'keeper whose daring did not in any way affect his utter reliability.
D. Lamming, *A Scottish Internationalists' Who's Who* 1987

JACK HARKNESS spent over 50 years associated with the game of football, firstly as an amateur with Queen's Park, becoming one of a select group of players to be capped at full level without having yet turned professional. He wore the goalkeeper's jersey with distinction for Scotland and also for Hearts who, although they never won any trophies, were a most popular team during the Twenties and Thirties. He then spent the remainder of his life as a football correspondent, prominently for the *Sunday Post*, covering Scotland's big matches at both club and national level. Jack Harkness was a well-known personality in the game throughout the years up to the 1980s.

From a generation that threw up an abundance of talented 'keepers, Harkness was one of the best – quick and brave and ever reliable. Both the Scottish and English leagues were littered with star names between the posts, and Scotland, a country which after the era closed was to be long criticised for lack of quality goalkeepers, had several noted custodians. Following a pre-war tradition left by Doig, Rennie and Brownlie, Bill Harper of Hibs was the country's first choice until Harkness entered the scene, while Celtic's tragic young 'keeper, John Thomson was every bit as good. Motherwell sang the praises of Allan McClory and St Johnstone had Alex McLaren. Partick Thistle thought John Jackson, nicknamed 'Jakey', the best around. In the south, England relied on big names in John Hacking, Ted Hufton and Birmingham City's Harry Hibbs. They could also call upon John Brown and Dick Pym. Meanwhile Ireland were well served by Cardiff's Tom Farquharson and the renowned Elisha Scott of Liverpool.

Harkness took over from McClory in Scotland's side in February 1927, at a time when selectors were searching for a new man to replace the ageing Harper. Jack was not yet 20, but had greatly impressed officials in Scottish League games with Queen's Park and in the England versus Scotland amateur international at Filbert Street, Leicester. That was the first ever amateur fixture between the two countries and the Scots, with seven Queen's Park men in their ranks, returned with a 4-1 victory. Jack was picked for the full international with Northern Ireland in February and had a satisfying début. Scotland won 2-0 and Harkness became one of the youngest players ever to appear for the Scots, and at the time the

Jack Harkness, the amateur in Scotland's ranks and one of the soundest goalkeepers of the era.

youngest since the turn of the century. It was the first of 11 appearances for his country. *The Bulletin* newspaper described him as "debonair" and Harkness quickly became popular with supporters, especially for his sporting and gentlemanly approach to the game.

Harkness hailed from the Govanhill district of Glasgow and was always destined for a career in football since his early days at Mount Florida School. He won local trophies for the school side and in 1922 was picked for the Scotland Boys' line-up to meet England at Chelsea. All told, he was capped on four occasions at that level and when at Queen's Park School he was a member of the team that won the Scottish Intermediate Shield. Harkness created a record in the process by keeping a clean sheet through to the final.

With such a bright juvenile background it wasn't a surprise when he was invited to wear the colours of his local club, Queen's Park. Harkness had been watched when appearing in the Battlefield Church League and worked his way through all four XIs of the Hampden Park Club; the Hampden XI, the Victoria XI, the Strollers and the Queen's Division One side. By December 1925 he had made his début in the Scottish League, in a match at Falkirk.

Jack at that time had little intention of turning professional. He was proud to be a member of a traditional institution like Queen's Park, with the famous motto of *Ludere Causa Ludendi*. Translated it means, appropriately, "The Game for the Game's sake", following strict amateur rules. Harkness confirmed that those rules were staunchly adhered to. He noted, "Never once during my whole career at Hampden did I ever receive as much as one penny in cash." He never claimed expenses either. Queen's Park had account arrangements with boot suppliers, with a restaurant and with a taxi firm. Everything was thought of and so expertly managed that there was no need for cash, and therefore never a hint of illegal payments breaking the amateur status. There were few perks – in fact probably only one: as members of the Hampden club, players could purchase stand seats for big games at the ground. Not even a complimentary ticket was handed out, but at least Harkness was guaranteed a place for all international and Cup final fixtures.

Jack became a regular for Queen's during 1926. They were a mid-table side at best – not surprisingly, they never threatened to win the Championship due to professional dominance elsewhere. But Queen's Park could attract the pick of amateur talent in Scotland and produced a sometimes perplexing team, capable of playing well against the better teams, notably Rangers, and poorly against less testing opposition. They were a typical Cup XI, inconsistent but able to turn on the style in a big match environment.

In season 1926/27 they finished in 12th position, one of the club's best placings since the First World War, and the following season they were stopped only at the last hurdle from reaching the Scottish Cup final. It was, as Harkness remembered, "a glamorous march into the semi-final". Queen's took care of Arthurlie and Morton in early rounds, then Kilmarnock after a replay. In the quarter-final with Partick Thistle, Harkness made sure his side went through with a series of excellent saves. They might have lost by four or five goals but for "the super work of Harkness", as one match report noted. Instead Queen's won 1-0 and met Celtic at Ibrox Park in the semi-final.

Celtic were a club Harkness had a fond association with. He had in fact appeared for the Celts a few months earlier in a challenge game at St James Park, Newcastle. At the time, Celtic boss Willie Maley had 'keeper problems, with both Shevlin and Thomson unavailable, and needed a sound goalie for what was a prestige meeting. So in stepped Jack Harkness, temporarily transferred to Celtic for a day. There was also another close connection between Harkness and the Green and Whites. Every other Saturday evening during the season there was a get-together between Harkness and Celtic's Jimmy McGrory and John Thomson at a corner table in the balcony of Green's Playhouse in Glasgow. They chatted all night about football, Harkness and Thomson on how they stopped goals and McGrory about how he found the back of the net. Thomson,

Jack at Wembley in 1928 being presented to the Duke of York, later King George VI.
Left to right: Gallacher, Jackson, Gibson, Harkness, Nelson, Bradshaw and skipper
McMullan.

in fact, was one of Harkness's closest friends and his tragic death in the Rangers versus Celtic derby, when only 23 years old, stood out as Jack's saddest moment in his 50 years in the game.

Over 54,000 witnessed a torrid semi-final encounter in which Celtic were described as "the luckiest team in the world". Queen's Park went down 2-1 but missed several clear-cut opportunities in a second period that saw Harkness a mere spectator. David Meiklejohn of finalists Rangers said to Harkness after the game, "I'll tell you something for nothing. We'd rather be meeting Celtic in the final than this Queen's Park lot." That was high praise indeed for the bunch of Hampden amateurs.

That week in March 1928 was quite a turning point in the career of Jack Harkness. Queen's Park's Scottish Cup run had given him the spotlight and a few days later he was travelling south to London as Scotland's goalkeeper to face England. It was Jack's second game against the Auld Enemy – he had appeared in the fixture at his home stadium a year earlier, a fabulous occasion for the Hampden-based player. But being part of the Wembley Wizards' victory was his proudest moment. He became on that celebrated afternoon the only amateur to play between the posts in a Home International fixture at Wembley.

Heart of Midlothian in 1928/29, including new signings Harkness, Bennie and Battles. It was Jack's first season as a professional. Back row, left to right: *William McCartney (manager), Herd, Shaw, Harkness, King, unknown, Bennie.* Front row: *Smith, Battles, Kerr, McMillan, Murray.*

Soon though, Harkness would be caught by the professional net. A 'keeper of his ability just could not remain an amateur for much longer. On his return to Glasgow negotiations opened for his transfer to Heart of Midlothian and within a month he had crossed the divide. Harkness met Hearts' boss Willie McCartney and immediately a relationship was struck. Jack was to say later, "They don't make managers like him any more." McCartney was big and portly and usually wore a carnation in his button-hole. He had a booming laugh and was a flamboyant character whom Harkness quickly took a liking to.

On 3 May 1928 Harkness turned professional and in doing so received the not inconsiderable £2,000 transfer fee, Queen's Park's amateur rules, of course, not allowing transfer income. Like Alan Morton before him, who also switched to professional status from Queen's Park, the 21-year-old Harkness suddenly experienced and appreciated a new financial status. He now earned £8 per week and Hearts also arranged a job out of football for him, with a petroleum company. He became the club's highest wage-earner.

Hearts were a club striving, together with the new force of Motherwell, to challenge Rangers and Celtic in Scottish football. In season 1927/28 they ended up in fourth position behind that trio and in Jack's ten years at Tynecastle, Hearts always seemed fated to end just out of the frame. They had not won the Championship for over 30 years, not since 1896/97, and they were not to succeed until a further 30 years had passed.

Still, Hearts had an entertaining line-up. Apart from signing Jack Harkness they also brought another international to Edinburgh – Bob Bennie, one of Scotland's most creative players. An established left-half for Airdrie, he cost £2,300. Meanwhile a new centre-forward called Bernard Battles was secured in readiness for the new season. Battles, to be nicknamed 'Barney', became a legendary figure in Gorgie for his striking rate in front of goal.

There was much expectation around Tynecastle for the new 1928/29 season. The ground was in the middle of major upgrading but a massive 18,000 turned up to see the new men in a public trial. When Hearts' three new signings made their débuts during August, the fixture list ensured that Harkness faced his old club, Queen's Park. All went well and the 'Boys in Maroon' won comfortably by 3-1. They blended together well. Battles grabbed the goals . . . 31 in League outings and a massive 74 in all matches, including five in one match for the Scottish League XI. Hearts topped the League during the early stages of the season but slipped in the New Year and allowed Rangers to lift the title by what was, in the end, a wide margin.

The following season saw Hearts go close to winning the Scottish Cup, but again they fell just short of success. They disposed of Clydebank, then faced two derby clashes with St Bernard's and Hibernian before meeting Dundee in the quarter-final. After a replay Hearts won 4-0 and travelled to meet Rangers in the semi-final at Harkness's favourite ground, Hampden Park. The clash was seen by 92,048, but the Ibrox XI were too slick on the day, winning 4-1 and ending Hearts' Cup dream.

One of the main reasons for Hearts' lack of success before and after the turn of the decade was the ever-changing personnel at Tynecastle. Harkness saw a stream of players coming and going, some of them highly talented and mostly internationals. Peter Kerr was the veteran captain, solidly built and superbly fit, while ex-Celtic and Scotland skipper Willie McStay arrived at Tynecastle in the latter days of his career. Two of Hearts' finest ever personalities played alongside Harkness, full-back Andy Anderson, nicknamed Tiger, and Alex Massie, an outstanding schemer who departed for a big fee to Aston Villa. Massie left an impression on Harkness. He noted in his memoirs: "He was one of

Scotland v England 1930 – after the Wizards the next Auld Enemy clash at Wembley.
England extracted some revenge by scoring five goals. Jack Harkness can only watch as
the ball hits the Scotland net. Tommy Law is the player in the foreground.

the finest footballing half-backs it has ever been my pleasure to watch."
Jack also added that Massie was quite a character and said, "I had more
fun in football during my friendship with Massie than at any other time
in my career."

Massie possessed a tremendous sense of humour but also a quick
temper. It was his anger that on one occasion took Harkness to court
after an encounter with Kilmarnock. The clubs had met at Rugby Park
in a rough match. At the time there was little love lost between the two
sets of players and fans; in the previous game in Ayrshire, Massie had
been sent off after a fracas with a Killie player. From the referee's whistle
onwards tackles were furious and the home crowd was in an aggressive
mood against Hearts and Massie in particular.

Not that it worried the Hearts midfielder. Harkness related that, "He
strolled through that game in all his greatness, and made it perfectly
obvious that he was treating the barrackers with the utmost contempt."
That of course didn't do much to improve the volatile atmosphere. As the
final whistle went Massie headed for the tunnel followed by Harkness. As
they entered the exit a Kilmarnock fan leaned over the wall and hurled
abuse at the Hearts pair. Massie exploded and threw a handful of mud
over the spectator and a rumpus started, with Harkness in the middle of

Jack in Hearts' line-up for the 1933/34 season. Back row, left to right: *Massie, Herd, Anderson, Harkness, O'Neill, Johnston (A.).* Front row: *Johnston (R.), Walker, Gardiner, Smith, Murray.*

a mass of arms, fists and angry voices. The sequel was that Massie was charged with assaulting the home supporter and summoned to appear at Kilmarnock Police Court. Harkness was a prominent witness and was required to attend as well. As it turned out, the case ended in everyone shaking hands and the ugly incident being classed as an accident!

Massie was one character at Tynecastle and there were more. In the forward line Alex Munro had a repertoire of tricks that delighted the crowd while Andy Black, John Johnstone, Willie Reid and Andy Herd were all capped by their country. So too was Dave McCulloch and during Jack's later days, a young forward by the name of Tommy Walker came into the side – he was to become Hearts' most famous son.

However, honours eluded them all. Hearts' defence, Harkness excepted, never matched their exceptional forwards. In season 1930/31, a season in which Battles grabbed 44 goals in only 35 league games and headed the scorers' chart, they finished in fifth place. They were third behind Rangers in both 1932/33 and 1934/35 and also reached the Cup semi-final, going down to the Ibrox club once more. Hearts, though, were thrilling to watch. In one typical match in September 1933 they found themselves 4-1 behind to Cowdenbeath at Tynecastle with only 20 minutes left. Battles then scored four and Hearts won 5-4. In a Scottish Cup-tie a year earlier they toppled Lochgelly United by all of 13-3 and on another occasion took care of arch-rivals, Hibs, 8-3 to the joy of half of the capital.

The Sunday Post, May 25, 1975 35

WEMBLEY *Special* **By Jack Harkness**

A SIX-MINUTE DISASTER!

ENGLAND 5, SCOTLAND 1.

(Half-time—3-1.)

Scorers:—England—Francis (4, 65 min.), Beattie (6), Bell (40), Johnson (75); Scotland —Rioch (pen. 41).

THE biggest tragedy of this defeat from Scotland's viewpoint was that the game was virtually over in six minutes. By that time we were two goals down—and the players hadn't even got used to the Wembley atmosphere.

We had only three players in this team remaining from our World Cup team of less than a year ago. And it showed.

Wembley has a certain mystique. No other ground in the world possesses this atmosphere. You need experience to cope with it. Scotland didn't have this quality.

So let's look at those two goals which meant so much.

England's Gerry Francis latched on to a stray ball fully 22 yards from the Scots goal. Francis hit it first time—and next thing—the ball was bulging the net behind Kennedy.

Maybe the goalkeeper was unsighted. Maybe he was unnerved. Anyway he made no effort to save.

You could still hear the silence from the Scots fans when England struck again. Once more surprise was the key note.

A harmless-looking cross from Keegan zeroed in on Beattie. A 10-yard header. This time Stewart Kennedy seemed to be taking a referendum on whether to stay in or come out!

And while the goalie was making up his mind, Beattie's header went sailing into the net at the top corner.

Two goals out of next to nothing. The game hardly started. No wonder this English team looked so delighted.

Anyway, from then on the game became almost a non-event. England, without showing any sustained brilliance, contented themselves with just pushing the ball around.

The Scots seemed too flabbergasted to do anything about it.

Yet there was one brief spell when we thought we were getting on top. A bit of pressure on England and the banners suddenly reappeared on the terracing. A goal could maybe have transformed the whole game.

I say "maybe." Because, lo and behold, it was England who broke loose and added No. 3.

Again there seemed no danger at the time. But Colin Bell seemed to run right through Danny McGrain before scoring the ball almost casually past Kennedy.

Straight from that goal the Scots careered upfield and were awarded a penalty after Todd handled. Bruce Rioch took the penalty kick and scored easily.

So, I ask myself—if Scotland had got that goal one minute earlier would the whole picture of this game have been altered? It would have made it 2-1 and maybe we could have come back as we did at Cardiff last week.

Maybe, though, I'm just kidding myself and indulging in a bit of wishful thinking.

Because, as it turned out, from then onwards it was no race. England just kept control and let the Scots do all the worrying.

Two-Goal Blast Put Scotland Down And Out

And a worried team they certainly did look.

As the game drew towards its close, England inflicted further indignities by indulging in quite a bit of mickey-taking. And, of course, they scored twice.

Number four came via Gerry Francis from a twice-taken free-kick.

And shortly afterwards Johnson made it five. A scrambling sort of goal following a goalmouth scrimmage after the ball had come down off the crossbar.

It was an unsatisfactory game from the purists point of view. Especially if you were a Scot.

Willie Ormond did try to alter the pattern when he sent on as substitutes Hutchinson and Macari for Duncan and McDougall.

I ADMIT TO BEING A BIT SURPRISED AT DUNCAN'S WITHDRAWAL. BECAUSE AT THE TIME I FELT THAT IF WE HAD ANOTHER FOUR DUNCANS UP FRONT, THINGS MIGHT HAVE BEEN A BIT DIFFERENT. HE WAS SHOWING REAL SPIRIT.

Five minutes from the end, England sent on Thomas for Keegan.

But by then they could have pulled off anyone and not bothered about sending on a substitute!

The most humbling point for Scotland does not stem so much from the beating as from the fact we were so easily whipped by a team that for long enough looked no great shakes themselves.

For a spell midway through the first half, we seemed to have plenty of ideas without the necessary "dig" to put them into effect.

I thought Alfie Conn was the one Scot to do himself justice.

But what happened to the usual flair of such accomplished players as Sandy Jardine and Kenny Dalglish I'll never know. They just couldn't get into the game.

I was truly sorry for Stewart Kennedy. He lost early goals before he had a chance to get his eye in, and his confidence suffered accordingly.

McGrain, McQueen and Munro, without being polished, played their hearts out, knowing, no doubt, they were fighting a lost cause.

England weren't a great team. They had the star man afield in Gerry Francis from Queens' Park Rangers. And other greats in Clemence, Todd, Watson, and Keegan. BUT NEVER SURELY HAS AN ENGLAND TEAM FOUND SO MUCH GOING FOR THEM WHILST EXPENDING SO LITTLE EFFORT.

STARS FOR MERIT

ENGLAND	SCOTLAND
**** CLEMENCE	** KENNEDY
*** WHITWORTH	** JARDINE
*** BEATTIE	*** McGRAIN
*** BELL	*** MUNRO
*** WATSON	*** McQUEEN
**** TODD	* RIOCH
*** BALL	** DALGLISH
** CHANNON	**** CONN
** JOHNSON	** PARLANE
***** G. FRANCIS	* MacDOUGALL
*** KEEGAN	** DUNCAN
*** THOMAS (sub.)	* MACARI (sub.)
	* HUTCHISON (sub.)

**** R. GLOECKNER, East Germany.

"Most Satisfying Win" — Revie

DON REVIE was unemotional after the 5-1 success. But he admitted, "We played very, very well, and this was the most satisfying win in my eight games as manager, without any shadow of a doubt. There was a lot of good football, and our shooting was on target."

Revie was pleased for his captain, Alan Ball. "He has been a wonderful servant, and this is one of the highlights of his career. I am delighted he was captain.

"I thought they all played well, and the balance of the side was better. We tried to bypass the Scots in midfield and bring people up in support of the front men.

"Keegan, Channon, and Johnson all showed willing right from the start, and Gerry Francis also did a good job."

During his time in charge, like Cyprus and Portugal. "Give me 16 players and I could also put up a good Revie has seen England struggle to score against teams defensive wall. At least the Scots came out and attacked."

And he'd a special word for Keegan, who earlier this week walked out on the England squad. "He never stopped running. He has got skill and guts, and anybody who marks him knows they have been in the game.

The start of Scotland's misery: 'Keeper STEWART KENNEDY looks on unhappily as the ball nestles in the back of the net after England's opening goal.

Records All The Way For Parker

COVENTRY'S David Parker, looking beyond this year's world championships to the Olympics in 1976, was right on schedule when he broke the English 1500 metres free-style record at Crystal Palace yesterday.

In the A.S.A.'s trials for the world championships in Cali, Colombia, in July, Parker finished three seconds within the qualifying time, reduced his own English record by ten seconds with a time of 16 min. 11.39 sec., and cut the English 800 metres record by 1.5 sec.

Parker reached 800 metres in 8 min. 41.1 sec.

Cardiff all-rounder, Ann Adams, who had already qualified in the women's 400 metres individual medley, took almost two seconds off the Welsh record with a time of 5 min. 11.39 sec. in that event today.

SWIMMING

The 15-year-old Welsh girl was the fastest of three to achieve the qualifying time, finishing ahead of European bronze medalist Sue Richardson, of Beckenham, and Scotland's Debbie Simpson.

Miss Richardson has spent the last six months in Australia following the European Championships but she was obviously out of touch and fell well short of that class of performance.

SHOW JUMPING

MALCOLM Pyrah, who hopes to challenge for an Olympic medal next year, scored another notable success with April Love at the Royal Windsor Horse Show yesterday.

The 34-year-old Yorkshireman, the first British showjumper to revert to amateur status following an appeal to the International Equestrian Federation, had his second win of the show with the Australian-bred mare when he won the Ranizole gamblers event.

Scoring 860 points, Pyrah's nearest challenger was Lionel Dunning, with 830 points on Arran Blaze. Dunnings wife, Pam, had 30 points fewer in taking third place on Sugar Plum.

Their success set the seal on a day of family success, for Mrs Dunning's 14-year-old cousin, Jane Smith, from Newark, had already won the junior championship with Mystery earlier in the day.

THE New Zealand cricket team to play in the Prudential World Cup one-day series in England next month left Auckland airport yesterday. Already playing county cricket in England are skipper Glenn Turner, Geoff Howart, John Parker, and David O'Sullivan.

They will practise at Eastbourne on May 31 and June 1 and 2 in preparation for their first match against East Africa at Edgbaston, Birmingham, on June 7.

HALIFAX Town may sign Tommy Veitch, former Tranmere and Hearts wing-half. Veitch is now playing with Chicago F.C. in the North American League, but will return home early in August.

BOYCOTT SHOCK FOR M.C.C.

GEOFF BOYCOTT, Yorkshire's 34-year-old captain, has opted out of next month's Prudential Cup and Test series against Australia later this summer for personal reasons.

Boycott informed Alec Bedser of his decision and then said, "For the first time in 18 months, I have found peace in cricket. I am now enjoying the game and do not want anything to upset the present trend. I regard my main task as that of leading Yorkshire back to cricket supremacy and the next two summers are going to be important. There is more to cricket than batting all day and getting plenty of runs."

Boycott's rejection of international cricket goes back a long way. He missed tours to Pakistan in 1968 and to India and Pakistan in 1972-73 for health reasons. Last June he stood down from the England team after one Test against India, and that was his last appearance for England.

He could not force his way back for the Pakistan series, and after being selected for the tour of Australia and New Zealand last autumn, he dropped out a month before departure.

Boycott's attitude certainly seems to be undergoing a change. The old Boycott thought nothing was more important than accumulating runs, but by missing overseas tours he had already showed that the runs available to him on good pitches were not so important to him.

Despite his inconsistent appearances at the highest level in recent seasons, Boycott is still acknowledged as England's best batsman. After the humiliation of England's other batsmen at the hands of Jeff Thomson and Dennis Lillee in Australia last winter, Boycott represented a slim hope that this ferocious pair could be mastered and the Ashes regained.

Yorkshire chairman John Temple said, "I am sorry and disappointed that Boycott has taken this decision. Throughout our proud history, Yorkshire have always encouraged their cricketers to play for England, but the decision is a personal one."

TENNIS

Second Title For Lesley

LESLEY CHARLES, the 22-year-old British number four, took just an hour—but needed eight match points—to gain her second singles title in a fortnight, when she won the Rothmans Surrey Hard Court Championship at Guildford. Miss Charles, who won the tournament at Lee-on-Solent, two weeks ago, defeated the 24-year-old Australian Cynthia Doerner, 6-3, 6-4 after dominating for all but a few shaky moments over the last two or three games.

Miss Charles got right away at the start by winning the first five games of the match and not until she led 5-3 and 40-love in the second set did she show signs of faltering.

Then five match points went begging before the Australian finally won that game only to trail love-40 again in the 10th.

Two forehand errors by Miss Charles then cost her her sixth and seventh match points before Mrs Doerner hit out on the eighth.

Peter Doerner, the husband of the losing women's singles finalist, also went down in his men's singles against the South African international, Byrom Bertram.

After leading 6-4, 4-1 and with two points for 5-2, Doerner, following a line dispute, faded right out of the match. Bertram took complete control with seven winning games in a row and went on to a 4-6, 6-4, 6-2 victory.

GEORGE FRANCIS, manager of John Conteh, the world light-heavy-weight boxing champion, has signed up Paul Kinsella, 19-year-old former national schools A.B.A. heavy-weight champion. Kinsella boxed for Kirkby B.C., Liverpool.

Harkness in a journalist role reporting on a big occasion, the England v Scotland clash of 1975.

Crowds came through the turnstiles in their thousands and only Rangers had better appeal. It was against the Light Blues in a 1932 Cup meeting that a record attendance of 53,396 packed into the Dalry stadium. For other games, gates averaged 20,000, regularly reaching 40,000 on a visit from Celtic, Rangers or Hibs. Harkness was remarkably consistent for the side, rarely missing a fixture. He was handed the title of 'Jack o'Hearts' and given a benefit match in 1934. Unfortunately it was a poorly supported tussle with Huddersfield Town. Harkness was one of the soundest 'keepers of the time, possessing all that a top goalkeeper needed. He was well built, almost five feet eleven inches and 11 stone. He possessed quickness of hand and eye with a sense of anticipation and a decisive mind. Not that he didn't make mistakes – like any goalkeeper he made errors, and they were usually costly and embarrassing, but they were few and far between. He is still Hearts' most-capped goalkeeper and appeared for the final time for Scotland in September 1933 at Parkhead against the Irish. The Scots lost 2-1 and Canadian Joe Kennaway took his place afterwards.

When aged 30, injury placed Harkness on the sidelines for the first time in his career. Knee damage took months of treatment and never really healed despite an operation and lots of therapy. This bad luck, on top of four broken fingers, made Harkness think hard about giving up the game before it left a permanent mark on his life.

He played his last senior match in football in August 1936, against Motherwell, a 4-3 defeat in which, with his leg still troubling him, he received some harsh criticism. It was Jack's 324th match for Hearts and the 440th in his career. By the end of the season he announced his retirement. Perhaps it was an opportune moment to depart from the Tynecastle set-up as that year there was much boardroom bickering within the club after boss McCartney left for Easter Road to take charge of Hibs.

Jack Harkness didn't leave the game altogether though. As well as being employed as a representative for Drybrough's Brewery, he was by the 1937/38 season compiling reports on Hearts games for the *Daily Express*. It wasn't an occupation which carried the Hearts directors' approval. They felt his comments could possibly upset former team-mates and, in an authoritarian style more at home in a latter-day communist regime, demanded that the Scottish League put an end to ex-players speaking their mind through newspaper articles. It did little to stop Harkness becoming a highly successful journalist.

He worked freelance throughout the years up to the Second World War and even as a company sergeant in the RASC during the hostilities he still covered football matches, including top wartime international fixtures. By then he had worked for the *Sunday Post* and in 1946 he was offered a full-time position with Scotland's traditional Sunday paper.

From that time on Harkness occupied a press-box seat at almost every football occasion in Scotland, many more in England and on the Continent too. He covered League Championship deciders, Cup finals, Scotland versus England meetings, top European football and the World Cup. Every major game for the next 30 years and more had a place reserved for J.D. Harkness. And he wasn't afraid to express his opinions, some of them strong in words condemning football's rulers. Following Scotland's infamous defeat by Paraguay in Sweden during the 1958 World Cup he wrote, "Scotland lost this game purely and simply because of the worst job of team selecting I have ever known." Harkness jetted around the world watching football, although some of the travel arrangements at times left a lot to be desired. One East German aircraft looked like "a crate fitted with an engine, a propeller, and a couple of wings. And the pilot must at one time have been the No 1 stunt man." His was a fascinating career, the envy of many football enthusiasts, despite some dubious flying machines.

Barlinnie Prison in Glasgow was another of Jack Harkness's ports of call once he hung up his boots – but only for the most honest of reasons. He was always willing to help out, being appointed honorary sports officer at the large jail. On Wednesday evenings he used to bring a few football personalities to talk to the inmates. Harkness was devoted to the game, no matter in whatever capacity. He became chief sports writer at the *Post* and in the New Year's honours list of 1971 was awarded the MBE for his services to football, honoured alongside the likes of Agatha Christie. Sadly, though, his proud day was overshadowed by the devastating Ibrox disaster. Harkness had little time to think about a forthcoming audience with the Queen and receiving his award, he was too busy relating the tragedy in which 66 people were killed in the Glasgow Old Firm meeting.

Harkness retired in 1977 and lived in Newlands, Glasgow, till his death in 1985. He was a man devoted to football to his final day.

JOHN DIAMOND HARKNESS MBE

Career Span: 1925 to 1937
Born: Govanhill, Glasgow, 27 September 1907
Died: Glasgow, 6 October 1985
Career: Queen's Park, 1925; Heart of Midlothian, 1928; Retired 1937
Club Honours: None
Full Internationals: 11 appearances, 1927-34
1926/27 v N. Ireland, England
1927/28 v England
1928/29 v Wales, N. Ireland, England
1929/30 v Wales, England
1931/32 v Wales, France
1933/34 v N. Ireland
Amateur Internationals: Two appearances, 1926-28
Schools Internationals: Four appearances, 1922-24

Note: Discrepancy has resulted in who kept goal for Scotland in the 1933/34 clash with Wales. Official records give Joe Kennaway, but most newspapers noted Jack Harkness. This would be Jack's last international appearance and 12th cap for Scotland if the official record is incorrect.

MATCH ANALYSIS

Season	Club	League app-gls	Cup app-gls	Scotland app-gls	Other represent-ative app-gls	Total app-gls
1925-26	Queen's Pk (Div 1)	20-0	2-0	—	—	22-0
1926-27	Queen's Pk (Div 1)	38-0	2-0	2-0	1-0	43-0
1927-28	Queen's Pk (Div 1)	35-0	6-0	1-0	1-0	43-0
1928-29	Hearts (Div 1)	36-0	1-0	3-0	—	40-0
1929-30	Hearts (Div 1)	34-0	7-0	2-0	—	43-0
1930-31	Hearts (Div 1)	35-0	2-0	—	—	37-0
1931-32	Hearts (Div 1)	37-0	3-0	2-0	—	42-0
1932-33	Hearts (Div 1)	36-0	7-0	—	—	43-0
1933-34	Hearts (Div 1)	36-0	4-0	1-0	—	41-0
1934-35	Hearts (Div 1)	38-0	7-0	—	—	45-0
1935-36	Hearts (Div 1)	38-0	1-0	—	—	39-0
1936-37	Hearts (Div 1)	2-0	—	—	—	2-0
Total		385-0	42-0	11-0	2-0	440-0

4

JIMMY NELSON ... THE ERRANT FOOTBALLER

A fast, dour back, who gives nothing away and is sound in every department.
Topical Times Annual, 1928

THERE ARE few players who have as well-travelled a career as Jimmy Nelson who sampled football in every home country of the United Kingdom. He trekked around the far corners of the nation; from Glasgow to Belfast, across the Irish Sea to Cardiff, then back north almost 350 miles to Tyneside. A return south followed, this time to Southend, and finally a journey westwards back to the principality, his adopted homeland.

Nelson was born in Greenock, alongside the Clyde estuary, just after the turn of the century, on 7 January 1901. His stay in Scotland did not last long though: the Nelson family soon moved to Ireland and settled in Belfast. Nelson, then, never really had a Scots upbringing but he still had a relish for the national game, football.

Jimmy started as a centre-forward with local juvenile sides just before World War One. As he matured he developed into a strapping teenager, five foot eight inches tall and well built at almost 12 stone. He played football for two local Belfast clubs, St Paul's and Glenarm, and moved back from the forward line to prove a commanding figure at centre-half, on occasion switching to the right-back position, his eventual role. Football for Nelson in those years was purely part-time and on an amateur basis. He worked as an apprentice boilermaker in the shipyards, like his full-back partner at Wembley in 1928, Tommy Law. But his football skills soon had talent spotters noting his name.

Immediately after the war, Crusaders, one of Ireland's oldest clubs, approached Nelson and the young Scot quickly signed for the Belfast outfit. Although not an Irish League side at that time (Crusaders did not enter league competition until much later, in 1949), they provided the first step for Nelson in a career in football. He developed rapidly playing for Crusaders, so much so that he was selected as captain of the Irish Alliance XI to face an England combination. Nelson was the brightest prospect in Ireland and many thought he would make the first team of some renowned club across the Irish Sea.

At that time, in 1920, politics and sectarian violence started to affect all parts of society in Ireland, which was not yet separated into north and south. Nelson was caught in the turmoil of rebellion against the London Government and religious hatred spilled on to the football field too. There was violence at the semi-final of the Irish Cup between Glentoran

Jimmy Nelson, pictured shortly after joining Cardiff City in 1921.

and Belfast Celtic at Windsor Park and then, at the replay at Cliftonville, a young man ran on to the pitch, drew a revolver and fired into the crowd. Civil war was soon to engulf the country and eventually southern Ireland broke away, became a republic and the Irish Free State set up. A break in football came too with Northern Ireland – the six counties of the Protestant north – forming its own association.

Despite having to live in the midst of all these troubles, Nelson's footballing talents matured even further. Irish selectors had his name on their list of possibilities for a full cap in the Home International Championship but officials were surprised and somewhat embarrassed when the committee were advised that Nelson was actually Scottish by birth! Nelson missed out on honours but his reputation was solid and Football League clubs were quick to tempt the full-back into a full-time professional career.

The move from Ireland must have come as a god-send to young Nelson. In August 1921 Cardiff City approached him and his suitcase was packed in double quick time for the journey to Ninian Park. Nelson was joining a club that had made a meteoric advance in football since the First World War, an almost overnight success. Season 1920/21 had been Cardiff's very first year in the Football League and they had immediately won promotion into Division One, from the Southern League to the First

Division to compete with the likes of traditional giants Everton, Newcastle United and Aston Villa all within 12 months. In a few seasons they were to progress even further to become a new power in the game.

In charge of the Bluebirds was Fred Stewart, a long-serving stalwart who had built up a fine side. He saw Jimmy Nelson as a talented right-back with a good turn of speed and judgement at clearing the ball. Nelson, then just out of his 'teens, had to be patient for an opportunity. He spent almost the whole of the new 1921/22 season in the reserves and could only watch as City chased the League Championship and had a good run in the FA Cup. He was blooded twice in League fixtures as Cardiff finished the season in fourth place and reached the quarter-finals of the Cup.

Nelson would quickly be part of more top-class action at Ninian Park. The following season Stewart gave the Scot his chance and the 21-year-old grabbed the opportunity. He teamed up with fellow Scot Jimmy Blair in the heart of the City defence. Blair was an experienced pro from Glenboig in Lanarkshire. He had been rated the best back in Scotland just before the war, when with Clyde and Sheffield Wednesday, and he had just been capped by his country. In years to come he was to form with Nelson an all-international defence for City. It was a partnership which was to serve the Welsh club well.

A League Championship medal passed Nelson by in 1923/24 by the narrowest of margins – precisely 0.024 of a goal! The Welsh club has never come closer to winning football's most prestigious domestic trophy and few clubs, if any, have been pipped at the post by such a slender margin. Nelson was an everpresent in the Bluebird's side that challenged Sunderland and Huddersfield Town for the title.

On the final day of the season, City were heading the table as they entered the field for the last fixture of the season against Birmingham at St Andrews. A good win would ensure silverware for Wales, a slip up would see Huddersfield Town, the team of the era, snatch the honour. Everything went wrong for Nelson and company. Ace goalscorer Len Davies missed an ever so crucial penalty and City drew 0-0, while Huddersfield won 3-0 against Nottingham Forest and lifted the trophy. Had Davies converted that penalty or had the Yorkshiremen only won 2-0, the title would have gone to Wales for the first time.

It had still been a marvellous season for the Ninian Park club, despite the last gasp disappointment. Cardiff were now recognised as one of the top clubs in the country with a squad of talented players few could equal. A contemporary writer of the day took the trouble to tally up City's international players ... they had no fewer than 17 capped men on their playing staff at one time during the Twenties. To nobody's surprise Wales was well represented. Half-back Fred Keenor, skipper of club and country, was a name that stood out above all others. He was an inspiring leader. Herbie Evans, his namesake Jack Evans, as well as forwards Len and Willie Davies also played for the Welsh, as did Jack Lewis. Harry Beadles and Jack Nicholls graduated to play for their country too.

Ireland was represented by goalkeeper Tom Farquharson, respected throughout the Football League. Paddy McIlveny, Tom Watson and Tom Sloan also played for the Irish. Sloan and Watson were both former Crusaders men like Nelson. Additionally two further Irish internationals, Bert Smith and George Reid, had recently been transferred.

Jimmy Blair was picked as captain of Scotland and, with Keenor, Cardiff could boast the rare distinction of having two international skippers in the same club side. They actually faced each other in the Wales versus Scotland clash in 1924 at Cardiff. The Scots also honoured ex-Celtic inside-left Joe Cassidy and Dennis Lawson, the former St Mirren winger. In February 1925 Jimmy Nelson joined the list, being selected to wear his country's blue jersey for the first time in the match at Tynecastle against Wales.

Nelson had performed consistently throughout seasons 1923/24 and 1924/25 and Scotland's selectors could not ignore him, despite his having played none of his football north of the Border. In fact when he stepped on to the Hearts pitch it was the very first time he had kicked a ball in any sort of organised football match in his native country. In opposition to Nelson were five of his Cardiff team-mates, Keenor, Nicholls, Beadles and both Willie and Len Davies. Scotland though were inspired by Hughie Gallacher and Nelson returned south with the satisfaction of a convincing 3-1 victory and a good personal display.

Jimmy regained his place for the clash with Northern Ireland in Belfast, another home-coming for the full-back. Once more he performed well in another win, this time by 3-0, and he was the only Anglo-Scot selected in the three-match international season. But come the all-important fixture with England at the end of the football year, Nelson was overlooked, mainly due to the fact that he played his football 400 miles south of Glasgow. His rivals for the right-back position in Scotland's side were Celtic's Willie McStay, the jovial and burly figure of Aberdeen's Jock Hutton and later Douglas Gray, the long-serving defender from Rangers. Nelson in fact did not get a call up for another three years.

The year 1925 had already been a special one for Nelson. Capped by his country and noted in some quarters as the best in Britain, the cool and reliable full-back was a major force in the side which reached the FA Cup final, the first of two visits to Wembley in the space of three years. Cardiff had to fight all the way to reach their first Cup final. They toppled Division Three side Darlington after three games, then disposed of Fulham and Notts County in close meetings before facing Leicester City at Ninian Park. The Welshmen won with the last kick of the game, a goal

Victory for Wales at Wembley in 1927. Jimmy Nelson (third from front) *follows his captain, Fred Keenor, and Billy Hardy down the Wembley steps.*

direct from a corner-kick by Willie Davies. Cardiff met Blackburn Rovers in a semi-final confrontation at Meadow Lane and won 3-1. All was set for a trip to Wembley Stadium and a meeting with Sheffield United.

The final was dubbed the meeting of 'Old Masters' Sheffield United, and 'New Hopefuls' Cardiff City. Nelson's side was above the Blades in

Cardiff's successful side in 1927. Back row, left to right: *Thirlaway, Fred Stewart (manager), Nelson, Davies, Farquharson, Sloan, Watson, Curtis.* Front row: *Hardy, Ferguson, Keenor, Irving, Parry, McLachlan.*

Division One but the Welsh team never reached the level of skill and form their fans were accustomed to witnessing in League action. Cardiff were a nervous lot from kick-off to the final whistle – surprisingly so for the number of experienced internationals in their line-up, but Wembley's unique atmosphere affects even the most seasoned professional. They lost 1-0, a goal which resulted after a fateful mistake by Harry Wake who let in England's outside-left Fred Tunstall to choose his spot.

Cardiff, though, were to return to Wembley and make amends. In 1927 South Wales, like many parts of industrial Britain, was an ailing society. Coal, steel, tin and engineering industries declined alarmingly and the Welsh valleys were in a depressed state. Cardiff City Football Club, however temporarily, made people forget their troubles as the Bluebirds brought the FA Cup to Wales for the first, and up to now, only time.

Aston Villa, Darlington, again, Bolton, the Cup-holders, and Chelsea all fell to City before they met giant-killers Reading in the semi-final at Molineux. Cardiff now had another noted Scot in their ranks, centre-forward Hugh Ferguson, who signed from Motherwell and who grabbed over 360 League goals in his career. It was Ferguson, who netted twice along with Wake, making up for his 1925 blunder, who sent Cardiff back to the Empire Stadium and the chance of making amends for two years earlier.

City travelled to Wembley in a gaily decorated charabanc adorned with a leek and red dragon flag. They fielded virtually the same defence as 1925, but now had a new forward line led by the dangerous Ferguson. Sam Irving had been signed from Dundee, while Billy Hardy, a long-serving Geordie, ran midfield with technical brilliance. Outside-left George McLachlan, who was in the running for the Wizards' match, was another new name. Cardiff's strength lay at the back where Nelson was, as past Scottish international Andy McCombie said, "a masterful defender, ice-cool and never flustered".

In front of 91,206 fans, a grim, close encounter with Arsenal took place as both sides aimed to have their name on the FA Cup for the first time. Nelson played the game of his life and one report of the day noted that he "had been a hero".

Cardiff City's finest hour came with what Arsenal captain Charlie Buchan described as "a gift goal". With 17 minutes left, Hugh Ferguson received the ball from a throw-in. The Scot went forward and tried a crack at goal from 20 yards with a low drive. Dan Lewis, Arsenal's goalkeeper, got his hands to the ball but tragically mistimed his catch. The ball hit his knees and bounced into the net with Len Davies following up to make sure the ball crossed the line. It was a classic example of the kind of luck that can win or lose a Cup final. Ironically Lewis was a Welshman.

That tragic slip was enough to give Cardiff the FA Cup. Jimmy Nelson followed skipper Fred Keenor up the famous Wembley steps to receive the trophy from King George V. Little did he know he would take the same steps as captain of another Cup-winning side before his days in the game were over.

Nelson was at the peak of his career. In seasons 1926/27 and 1927/28 he created a club record at Ninian Park, clocking up 87 consecutive appearances. Jimmy was unruffled and uncompromising, but also a stylist and perfectionist. The *Topical Times* annual of the era noted, "A fast, dour back, who gives nothing away and is sound in every department", while another pen picture described Nelson as "a deadly tackler with rare powers of anticipation . . . adept at placing the ball properly". He had developed into a right-back of distinction, a must for Scotland, said all in the Football League. Nelson, however, was very much an Anglo and suffered for it, even though he had his supporters in the Scottish FA's headquarters in Glasgow. He was petitioned for a Scotland place by the respected press, and surprisingly so, on both sides of the Border. Established backs Hutton and McStay were at the time being criticised for their "lack of mobility". In March 1928 he

Nelson's last international fixture for Scotland against France in 1930. Back row, left to right: *Nelson, Thomson, Wilson, Walker, Hill, Crapnell.* Front row: *Jackson, Cheyne, Gallacher, Stevenson, Connor.*

was chosen for the international trial match at Firhill and he played himself into the line-up for the meeting with England with a sound, if not spectacular, performance. Nelson returned to Wembley and faced Huddersfield Town's Billy Smith, along with Hulme, one of England's speed merchants. The result of the confrontation was an overwhelming triumph for the full-back.

Nelson only played once more for Scotland after that Wizards' victory. To the annoyance of Cardiff supporters and the great surprise of many judges in the game, he was not picked again until he was in the party to play France in Paris during May 1930, when aged almost 30. Unluckily the banning of Anglos meant his international career was over. In his four games though, Scotland won each match convincingly: 3-1, 3-0, 5-1 and 2-0.

Glory days were far from over for Jimmy Nelson however. Immediately following the international in Paris, he was signed by Newcastle United's boss Andy Cunningham, the ex-Scotland schemer, who was looking for an experienced defender to bolster his club's rear-guard. United had to pay £7,000, a hefty fee for an ageing star but it proved to be money more than well spent.

The last few seasons at Ninian Park, although good for Nelson, who was as consistent as ever despite a long-term injury, were not rewarding for the club. Cardiff declined alarmingly following their FA Cup win, so much so that in 1928/29 they dropped back into Division Two. Remarkably perhaps, they were relegated with the best defensive record in the First Division with only 59 goals conceded. After a season of Second Division football, the Scot jumped at the chance of returning to Division One with Newcastle United.

Nelson joined the Magpies at a controversial time. Tyneside was still buzzing with anger over the sale to Chelsea of Hughie Gallacher, the centre-forward Nelson had played alongside a couple of weeks before, in the international in Paris. By the time Nelson had pulled on the black'n'white shirt for the first time at St James Park, Gallacher-fever had struck the city. The first home game of the season was against Gallacher and his new club, Chelsea. A record crowd flocked to Newcastle's Gallowgate stadium to witness the return of their former idol. It was an extraordinary home début for Nelson, one he remembered distinctly, especially when he badly twisted a knee minutes after the interval and had to hobble off to the treatment table. Through cartilage trouble Jimmy missed the next 14 games for his new club, hardly the sort of start he was looking for.

Once fit again, however, Nelson showed the Geordie public what an accomplished full-back he was. He hardly missed a game for the next three-and-a-half seasons. Appointed skipper, he also returned to Wembley, leading United in the FA Cup final of 1932. It was an occasion, along with the Wizards' match that was the highlight of his distinguished career.

Nelson's experience was invaluable in the Magpies' triumph over Arsenal, a side at the height of their Thirties' ascendancy. The Londoners were forced to leave out fellow Wembley Wizard Alex James due to injury, but they still had enough stars to swamp Newcastle, on paper at least. Few gave Nelson's men a chance against the polished talents of the men from Highbury.

United had, though, a few personalities of their own. Apart from Nelson, other notable Tynesiders were goalkeeper Albert McInroy, who with inside-forward Jimmy Richardson and the powerful Sammy Weaver played for England. Weaver, famed for a prodigious throw, was a phenomenon of the era. Scotland was further represented by Jimmy Boyd, capped in the months ahead and an ex-St Bernard's product. The team was littered with other Scots too – Tommy Lang, Dave Davidson, Roddie McKenzie and Harry McMenemy, from a famous footballing

Approaching the veteran stage, Jimmy joined Newcastle United in 1930 and proceeded to have a marvellous association in a black'n'white shirt.

Newcastle United v Arsenal, 1932 FA Cup final. Nelson and David Jack in a tussle for the ball.

family. Local favourite Jack Allen was the danger man up front, and the centre-forward went on to hog the headlines with two goal strikes to give the Tynesiders the Cup in what was a highly controversial match, to become known as "The Over the Line Final".

Nelson had been involved in the opening goal when Bob John put Arsenal ahead. The Newcastle captain, uncharacteristically, was involved in a mix-up with goalkeeper McInroy that led to the Arsenal player nipping in between them and heading into the net. Then came Newcastle's 38th minute equaliser, a goal still talked about to this day. Davidson sent Richardson down the wing in pursuit of a long, raking pass. He whipped the ball across from the by-line and there was Allen to take advantage of a moment's hesitation in the Gunners' defence. A goal it was, but what a rumpus it caused . . . perhaps the most controversial goal in the history of the FA Cup. After the game the media, including the *British Movietone* newsreel of the day, showed that the ball had crossed the by-line before Richardson had centred the ball. It was clearly out of play and the goal should not have stood.

From that debatable moment, Nelson marshalled his side and took control of the game. Allen scored the winner near the end after beating

Victory at Wembley for a third time. As Newcastle skipper, Nelson received the trophy from Queen Mary.

two defenders to allow Jimmy Nelson the honour of climbing those Wembley steps once more, this time leading his side as captain. Queen Mary handed over the trophy and Nelson had again seen off Arsenal, a repeat of Cardiff's victory five years earlier.

Now approaching the veteran class, Nelson played on with the Magpies for three seasons but, as with Cardiff, saw his club slip dramatically after success. United were relegated after 36 years' unbroken service in Division One and in June 1935 Jimmy was on his travels again, this time on yet another long trip, to Southend United.

Managed then by the accomplished ex-Bolton and Arsenal star, David Jack, Southend provided Nelson with his final fling, in the unglamorous stage of Division Three (South) football. He played until he was 38 years of age, when the outbreak of World War Two put an end to a first-class career of over 500 games and which spanned two decades. Yet Nelson continued into his 40th year, playing wartime games for Ekco Sports in Southend, always showing that the motto that had followed him around of "steady and always ready" was a fitting description of his play.

He assisted the Shrimpers for some years, also running a local public house, the Plymouth Hotel, before moving back to South Wales, to Penarth on the Severn estuary. Football was always to remain close to Nelson. His son Tony became a noted player for Newport County and Bournemouth. He was good enough to be capped by Wales at amateur level in 1952. His son-in-law, Stan Montgomery, was recommended to his old club, Cardiff City, by Nelson in 1948 and he went on to have a distinguished career with the Blues, as well as being a fine Glamorgan cricketer.

Nelson continued in the licensed trade, running the Greyhound Inn on the outskirts of Cardiff until his death in 1965. Tales of football were commonplace, not surprising for a man who had been to Wembley for the biggest occasions on the football calendar . . . FA Cup finals, three of them, and the most famous England versus Scotland match ever.

JAMES NELSON

Career span: 1921 to 1939
Born: Greenock, 7 January 1901
Died: Sully, near Barry, 8 October 1965
Career: Belfast Crusaders; Cardiff City, 1921; Newcastle United, 1930; Southend United, 1935; Ekco Sports, 1939; Retired 1945
Club Honours:
FL Championship Runner-Up, 1924
FA Cup Winner, 1927, 1932
FA Cup Runner-Up, 1925
Welsh FA Cup Winner, 1923, 1927, 1928, 1930
Full Internationals: Four appearances, no goals, 1925-30
1924/25 v Wales, N Ireland
1927/28 v England
1929/30 v France

MATCH ANALYSIS

Season	Club	League app-gls	Cup app-gls	Scotland app-gls	Other represent- ative app-gls	Total app-gls
1921-22	Cardiff City (Div 1)	2-0	0-0	—	—	2-0
1922-23	Cardiff City (Div 1)	17-0	3-0	—	—	20-0
1923-24	Cardiff City (Div 1)	42-0	6-0	—	—	48-0
1924-25	Cardiff City (Div 1)	37-2	8-0	2-0	—	47-2
1925-26	Cardiff City (Div 1)	34-0	3-0	—	—	37-0
1926-27	Cardiff City (Div 1)	38-0	7-0	—	—	45-0
1927-28	Cardiff City (Div 1)	41-0	3-0	1-0	—	45-0
1928-29	Cardiff City (Div 1)	11-0	0-0	—	—	11-0
1929-30	Cardiff City (Div 2)	18-0	0-0	1-0	—	19-0
1930-31	Newcastle Utd (Div 1)	23-0	2-0	—	—	25-0
1931-32	Newcastle Utd (Div 1)	40-0	9-0	—	—	49-0
1932-33	Newcastle Utd (Div 1)	40-0	1-0	—	—	41-0
1933-34	Newcastle Utd (Div 1)	40-0	1-0	—	—	41-0
1934-35	Newcastle Utd (Div 2)	3-0	0-0	—	—	3-0
1935-36	Southend Utd (Div 3)	37-0	4-0	—	—	41-0
1936-37	Southend Utd (Div 3)	24-0	4-0	—	—	28-0
1937-38	Southend Utd (Div 3)	9-0	0-0	—	—	9-0
1938-39	Southend Utd (Div 3)	3-0	0-0	—	—	3-0
Total		459-2	51-0	4-0	—	514-2

5

TOMMY LAW . . . THE UNKNOWN BABE

The most brilliant player produced by Chelsea for a long time.
The Times, March 1928

JIMMY NELSON'S full-back partner at Wembley Stadium was another player who was very much an Anglo, and another who hardly kicked a ball in Scotland. Tommy Law, unlike Nelson who in 1928 was recognised by Scots fans as a reputable and able defender, had also to suffer the ignominious situation of being almost totally unknown north of the Border. At the time Law was hardly 20 years of age and had just completed his first season in Chelsea's League eleven, in a side that was struggling to gain promotion from English Second Division obscurity.

Tommy Law, though, had a rapid elevation to fame. *The Times* noted in 1928 that he was "the most brilliant player produced by Chelsea for a long time". Within the space of a year and a half he had made his début in senior football, displaced established Chelsea full-back Fred Barrett, become a regular in the side, and had then caught the eye of Scottish selectors with a series of outstanding performances. He was picked for Scotland's international trial in March 1928 and faced St Johnstone's winger, Gavigan. Another top-quality display nudged the officials to pick him for a full cap in the prestigious Scotland versus England encounter two weeks later. From being a raw Scottish teenager, an unknown budding footballer miles away from home, Tommy Law was plunged into the very top stage of the game, representing his country in the match of the year. And he never looked back.

Law had displaced Willie McStay of Celtic, a noted and versatile international, who played in both full-back positions for Scotland and had captained the national eleven. He had quite a task in front of him, having to face, at Wembley, England's 'Highbury Express', Joe Hulme. Grave doubts were expressed about whether Law had the experience and ability for such a testing opposition and emotive occasion. The doubters though had no cause for concern. Law performed quite brilliantly for a player so young on his début. He blended perfectly with his left-half partner, Jimmy McMullan, and as for danger-man Hulme, well, the Arsenal winger never got a look-in. The babe in the side had passed his test with an accomplished afternoon's work.

Tommy Law hailed from Glasgow and was born, for his troubles, on April Fool's Day 1908. He was one of football's late developers, never being a budding star at school in Finnieston. Law did not really take

Tommy Law pictured in 1928, a youngster who had just reached the big-time.

to the game until he left the classroom and was spotted kicking a ball around, by enthusiasts who ran Claremont Union, a junior side playing in the Glasgow Churches League. He was an outside-left in those days but soon settled in defence where his stocky 12 stone, five-foot-nine-inch frame was ideally suited for a left-back role.

Claremont was very much one of Glasgow's subordinate local sides and Law stood out in this class of football during the early years of the Twenties. Bridgeton Waverley were a club of higher standing and they took the full-back into a better grade of football where his rise to the top was literally overnight. Law had only played all of five games for his new club before Chelsea scouts had spotted that the young Scot had abundant natural skills. A report was quickly posted to Stamford Bridge and officials in Scotland were given the nod to snap the youngster up. Within the space of weeks, in the Spring of 1925, Law had graduated from Glasgow church football to the English Football League and to one of the biggest clubs in the game.

Law quit his job as a boilermaker in a Clydebank shipyard and headed for London. From those Clyde yards in the midst of depression, Law found himself in the relatively prosperous south, the capital and a rich society. He was a stranger, a northerner at that, and only 17 years of age, in a vast urban area with a notoriously cold heart. It was quite an ordeal

Andy Wilson, the former Scotland centre-forward who was a great influence at Stamford Bridge.

and Law was uncomfortable about the prospect, but soon familiar voices welcomed the youngster to Stamford Bridge.

Chelsea at that time, and throughout the long period Law stayed with the 'Pensioners', had a big Scots influence. In charge was David Calderhead, a former Scotland international who had appeared prominently as skipper of the Notts County side which had reached two FA Cup finals and who was capped in 1889 when with Queen of the South Wanderers. He never concealed his liking for the ball skills associated with players from his homeland and brought plenty of his own countrymen to Stamford Bridge. It was very much a Scots retreat, ideally suited for a teenager miles from Glasgow and away from a family environment for the first time.

Another influence at Stamford Bridge when Law joined the staff was Andy Wilson, Scotland's centre-forward who netted 17 goals in 14 internationals during the years following World War One. Wilson, a native of Lanarkshire, was one of the biggest personalities of the game, both north and south of the Cheviots divide. He had broken the transfer record when he moved from Middlesbrough to Chelsea for £6,000 in 1923. He had also played for Hearts and assisted Dunfermline in the rebel Scots Central League. Small and burly, but with a consummate touch on the ball, Wilson overcame a shattered arm injury received while on military service in the First World War. Both Wilson and boss

Calderhead were important factors in the quick development of Law.

Chelsea had just been relegated from the English First Division a year before Law signed for the princely sum of £10. They were eager for an immediate return to the fold but found the Second Division a difficult class of football to be rid of. They were not the first or last so-called big club to have encountered the same problem. In season 1925/26 the 'Pensioners' made all the promotion running until the very end of the season then slipped up to finish third. Tommy Law didn't get into the first-team action that year, instead being content with learning the professional game in the London Combination League with other reserve sides of the capital. He visited all the top grounds – Highbury, White Hart Lane, Upton Park – but was soon to be given his chance to grace those stadiums in first-class football.

Calderhead picked Law, now 18 years old, for a League baptism in Chelsea's trip to face Bradford City on 18 September 1926. He partnered George Smith at full-back, in what was to be the start of a formidable tartan defensive partnership at the Bridge. Smith was from Parkhead and played alongside Law for the next few seasons. They were two of five Scots in Chelsea's line-up at Valley Parade, others being John Priestley, ex-St Johnstone, Robert Turnbull from Dumbarton, and Willie Ferguson who had arrived from Calderhead's old side in Dumfries. Andy Wilson would have made it six, but he was injured.

Chelsea defeated Bradford City 1-0 to cap a bright opening for Law in senior football. He played well and remained in the side, not missing a single game for the rest of the season, including an FA Cup run to the sixth round. It was the start of a long association with the Blues. Law remained a loyal servant to Chelsea for all his playing career . . . a one-club man.

Chelsea once more missed out on promotion, finishing in fourth place, and they did it yet again in 1927/28, the year Law caught the eye of Scottish selectors. Sandy-haired Tommy was always a player of the gentlemanly type but he was a fierce tackler and forwards knew they had been in a game when they came up against him. He was noted for a famous sliding tackle as much as James and Gallacher were famed for their dribbling. Past Chelsea historian, Ralph Finn, remembered the Law tackle in the Wizards' match. He wrote: "I can see him now, going down on his backside inside his own penalty area, and sliding over that slippery Wembley turf, polished by rain, a distance of about 20 yards to the touch-line to take the ball clearly from a surprised winger's feet." The crowd loved to see Law's outstretched leg clip the ball to safety and they rose to his fine passing ability too. He was from an era when most ordinary defenders cleared their lines with a hefty, aimless boot upfield. Law always tried to find a

Chelsea in 1928, a season the Londoners just failed to achieve promotion. Back row, left to right: *Miller, Priestley, O'Dell, Millington, Townrow, Wilding, Jackson.* Front row: *Law, Biswell, Ferguson, Wilson, Anderson, Pearson.*

colleague and many attacks stemmed from his ideas and vision at the back.

If Tom had one weakness it was a lack of pace but he concealed the deficiency with an acute sense of positional awareness. He was one of the best in the country at left-back and one profile of the Twenties declared Law "a top rate defender with few superiors", while another described him as "the essence of coolness".

Following Law's performance at Wembley for Scotland in 1928 he became one of the élite of London's sporting fraternity, elevated into the star bracket. Chelsea, though, had a disappointing year in 1928/29, never getting close to that ultimate goal of First Division football. At the end of the season Law was one of a party of 26 Chelsea players and officials that set sail on board the liner MS *Asturias* for a tour of Argentina, Uruguay and Brazil, a pioneering trip to South America. Law headed into one of the most sensational tours of all time which featured angry mobs, fiery matches, abandoned games, blatantly biased refereeing and even playing when revolver shots were being discharged from the crowd. Events became so bad that the local police chief warned Chelsea officials it would be inadvisable for the Blues to score a goal! They were also held in quarantine in Buenos Aires because of a yellow-fever epidemic. All in all it was an experience Law wanted to get away from quickly. Just as today, South American football was very much different from the set-up back in England.

The following season, at the sixth attempt, Chelsea at last got their promotion plan right. They finished runners-up to Blackpool and returned to Division One after so many near misses. Law was absent for only one game and had proved as consistent a performer as he had done in the previous three seasons. The Londoner's defence was the key to the club's success. Law and Smith were a strong duo behind a fine international half-back line. Sam Irving was capped by Northern Ireland and had played with Jimmy Nelson at Cardiff, while Sid Bishop and Jack Townrow were two cultured England players. Bishop would have faced Scotland at Wembley in 1928 but for illness. It was touch and go whether Chelsea would be successful but on the last day of the season, although defeated at Bury, their nearest rivals, Oldham Athletic, lost too, and Chelsea were up.

Law was recalled to the Scotland side at the end of the season, and with it came a return to the Empire Stadium. The game against England was Scotland's first back in front of the twin towers since 1928 and much was expected of the Scottish XI. However England exacted a degree of revenge and Tommy Law in particular suffered from an England winger on top form. It wasn't Joe Hulme, but his rival for the outside-right position, Sammy Crooks of Derby County. Four of England's five goals started from the Geordie winger. Law chased Crooks all afternoon but rarely got close to his heels. It was a game Law, and the legions of Scots fans, wanted to forget quickly.

In fact it was Law's last appearance in a national jersey. Scotland afterwards picked Joe Nibloe of Kilmarnock or Airdrie's, and later Motherwell's Jimmy Crapnell in the left-back position. Although his performance against Crooks did Law's reputation no good, the ultimate reason for his isolation from international football in the coming years was a controversy to be known as the "Anglo-Scots dispute".

A club versus country row blew up in the Thirties as clubs began following the English Football League's decision allowing them not to be obliged to release players for Irish, Welsh or Scottish international matches if fixtures clashed with League games, although, importantly, they still had to release players for England fixtures. With so many Anglos in the south it affected the Scots' team selection dramatically. Scottish officials were quite naturally aggrieved, as were their counterparts in Ireland and Wales, and they made a bold decision to overlook Anglo-Scots and pick home-based players. Out of international reckoning went the likes of Gibson, McMullan, James, Gallacher and Jackson. Out went Tommy Law too. In fact the list of quality talent from Scotland playing in the Football League was exceptional. Law had to be content with his two international caps, both for games at Wembley Stadium.

For their return to the First Division, Chelsea hit the headlines in a big way. The club was determined to make an impression now they were back with the élite. Money appeared to be no problem as Chelsea purchased well-known names in a bid to buy success. First to arrive was none other than Law's Wizard colleague, Hughie Gallacher. He was signed from Newcastle United in a £10,000 deal, just short of a new record fee. Next, £6,000 was spent on another Scottish international, Aberdeen's Alec Cheyne, then Alec Jackson sensationally arrived at Stamford Bridge for £8,500. Three Wembley Wizards in their line-up – Chelsea fans could hardly believe it.

Huge crowds flocked to south-west London, with over 75,000 there for a tussle, with rivals Arsenal smashing the attendance record. Stars galore were on view. Also to wear the Chelsea blue then were England's half-back Harold Miller and winger Jackie Crawford. More capped players arrived in the seasons ahead. Peter O'Dowd, Dick Spence and Vic Woodley all played for England too, along with Sammy Weaver, Nelson's team-mate at Newcastle who came south in another big transfer. From Rangers came Bob Macauley while Alan Craig, ex-Motherwell, joined the set-up, as did gifted winger Peter Buchanan. 'Keeper John Jackson was purchased from Partick Thistle. He was the eighth Scottish international to be at the Bridge during Law's stay there.

London's Scottish community, vast even then, not surprisingly swarmed to watch Chelsea. Expectation that Chelsea would challenge for honours was high in the capital. However results were disappointing and all this despite a team of quality players. They possessed dazzling individual talents but were unimpressive in a team combination. Tommy Law had a good season in 1930/31, becoming the team's penalty expert, crashing home seven spot-kicks that season in net-bursting style.

It was much the same story for the next few seasons at Stamford Bridge. The team never blended together although they almost reached the FA Cup final of 1932 before going out to Newcastle United in the semi-final at Leeds Road, Huddersfield. That was the nearest Tommy Law came to winning a domestic honour in his 15 years at Chelsea.

A season of problems followed that almost shook the very foundations of Stamford Bridge as player power challenged football's then antiquated and restrictive system. With so many moody stars in the dressing-room, morale and discipline were never very good. Management and players clashed frequently. They clashed over training, at their off-the-field activities, over Player Union membership – then not a popular organisation with the establishment – and over money, the root of all Chelsea's problems.

*Law in action during a London derby meeting with Arsenal in 1931. David Jack (left)
is fiercely tackled by Law.*

Top Chelsea players, including Law, were incensed at the maximum-
wage rule which then gave earnings of between £7 and £8 per week,
dropping to £6 in the summer months. Men like Law, Gallacher, Wilson
and Cheyne wanted more than the maximum. They reckoned, and rightly
so, that they drew fans to Stamford Bridge and deserved a share of the
profits. They, of course, lost their stand (as related in Alec Jackson's
profile, Chapter 9) but drew much attention and with it offers from the
Continent.

Law and Gallacher were jointly approached by French club Nîmes.
Officials met the Scots at a plush London hotel and the pair, as Gallacher
related, negotiated a lucrative package which was agreed without much
hesitation. They were to receive a £3,000 signing-on fee, £20 per week
and a three-year contract. In time, though, to Law's undoubted regret,
the deal fell through, although other Chelsea stars – Wilson and Cheyne
– did leave for deals in French soccer.

The following season Chelsea had an awful time, not surprisingly with
so much internal turmoil. They cheated the drop into Division Two by

69

Tommy Law later in his career.

a whisker and then appointed a new manager in 1933, the experienced Leslie Knighton. But it mattered little as another relegation battle ensued for Law and company.

Now the Blues' captain, a bad injury saw Law out of action for 18 months and Chelsea missed his influence. He was back for the 1935/36 season and his return coincided with a Chelsea revival. They finished in a modest eighth position, but by their standard it was a good season – a remarkable fact considering that in the inter-war period Chelsea fielded in excess of 20 full international players.

Now 30 years old, Law's days as a regular in Chelsea's line-up were limited. He played his last senior game in 1938, a home clash with Blackpool. He remained on the Chelsea staff as the senior influence on the reserve side but he was way past his best. One supporter at the time recalled Law as "a squat, almost tubby figure always short of pace". He stayed in the back stage of Stamford Bridge until just before the outbreak of World War Two, being granted a free transfer in May 1939.

Law had clocked up 321 games for the Londoners and few players have appeared more or served the club so well. As a player, Tommy Law's strength lay in his wonderful positioning and in his ability to make time to assess situations. He lived in London and watched his old club frequently. He was instantly recognisable in the Stamford Bridge stand. He died in February 1976 when 68 years of age.

THOMAS LAW

Career Span: 1925 to 1939
Born: Glasgow, 1 April 1908
Died: London, 17 February 1976
Career: Bridgeton Waverley; Chelsea, 1925; Retired 1939
Club Honours:
Football League Division Two Promotion, 1930
Full Internationals: Two appearances, no goals, 1928-30
1927/28 v England
1929/30 v England

MATCH ANALYSIS

Season	Club	League app-gls	Cup app-gls	Scotland app-gls	Other represent-ative app-gls	Total app-gls
1926–27	Chelsea (Div 2)	36-0	5-0	—	—	41-0
1927–28	Chelsea (Div 2)	38-1	1-0	1-0	—	40-1
1928–29	Chelsea (Div 2)	39-1	4-1	—	—	43-2
1929–30	Chelsea (Div 2)	41-0	1-0	1-0	—	43-0
1930–31	Chelsea (Div 1)	27-6	5-1	—	—	32-7
1931–32	Chelsea (Div 1)	27-1	7-2	—	—	34-3
1932–33	Chelsea (Div 1)	33-2	0-0	—	—	33-2
1933–34	Chelsea (Div 1)	25-4	2-0	—	—	27-4
1934–35	Chelsea (Div 1)	0-0	0-0	—	—	0-0
1935–36	Chelsea (Div 1)	23-0	1-0	—	—	24-0
1936–37	Chelsea (Div 1)	0-0	0-0	—	—	0-0
1937–38	Chelsea (Div 1)	4-0	0-0	—	—	4-0
Total		293-15	26-4	2-0	—	321-19

6

JIMMY GIBSON . . . A CLASSIC TALENT

The greatest natural footballer of modern days.
The Bulletin, March 1928

SCOTLAND'S DEMOLITION of England in 1928 was attributable to several factors, one significant element being the quality of the half-back line. Commentators described them with superlatives and the *Glasgow Herald* noted that the trio "gave an exhibition of half-back play that has rarely been equalled". Jimmy Gibson was right-half at Wembley on that day. A tall, lean, fair-haired figure with perpetual energy, he had the ability to capture the ball from opponents, set up attacks with intelligent passes and also go past markers at will.

Gibson was from a family of footballing stars and not many such households in the game can boast the array of honours held by the Gibsons of Larkhall. The game has witnessed many footballing families on grounds from Pittodrie to Anfield and Fratton Park – few, though, are of the pedigree of Jimmy Gibson, his two brothers, and illustrious father, Neil Gibson. A magnificent haul of caps and medals came their way. By the time Neil Gibson's sons had completed their careers in the game he was a very proud father indeed.

Jimmy and his elder brothers had quite a reputation to follow. Their father, Neil, was one of Scottish football's early masters, among the greatest names in the Edwardian era. A clever schemer, he was spotted in junior football by Rangers in 1894 and went on to have a marvellous association with the Ibrox club. Neilly, as he was commonly known, won Championship medals in 1899, 1900, 1901 and 1902, while he also reached four Cup finals and was on the winning side on three occasions. He possessed near perfect distribution and Scotland made him a regular in their line-up. He won 14 caps altogether and 11 Scottish League representative honours. He ended his career at Partick Thistle just before the Great War but Neilly Gibson's sons were soon following in their father's tradition.

Willie Gibson joined Ayr United and had a successful stay on the west coast before Newcastle United stepped in with a £2,500 bid in November 1923. A midfielder too, a year later he helped the Magpies to a Cup victory and then proved a vital link in the Tynesiders' Championship success of 1927, playing behind Hughie Gallacher. He was unlucky not to be capped when at St James Park and later held the Birmingham City trainer's post for many years.

Jimmy Gibson, a Partick Thistle star who moved south like many Scottish League players of the era.

Neil Gibson junior never made the well-worn passage south as did brothers Willie and Jimmy. Instead he remained for all of his career in Scotland. As a half-back, he was a loyal servant to Clyde for all of 11 seasons from 1923 to 1934 and was a respected Scottish League player.

While both Willie and Neil junior had exceptional club careers it was the youngest of the family, Jimmy Gibson, who rose to international fame as his father had done before him. Jimmy was born in Larkhall, as all the family were, and possessed similar ability to his brothers; they were all confident on the ball and had the capacity to stroke passes around at ease. But Jimmy oozed that extra touch of finesse. It was the natural footballer in him, his father's special talent.

It was with Partick Thistle, the club Neilly Gibson had ended his career with, that Jimmy made his name. Thistle officials knew the family's worth and made swift moves to capture Jimmy from junior club Glasgow Ashfield in May 1921. Gibson had starred for Ashfield,

Jimmy's father, Neilly Gibson, a Rangers and Scotland legend.

one of Scotland's most distinguished junior sides and a former League outfit. He played in the 1921 Junior Cup final at Hampden, against his previous team, another noted non-league combination, Kirkintilloch Rob Roy. Ashfield lost 1-0 but Gibson had impressed watching scouts in the 26,000 crowd and was, within a few short weeks of that game, signing professional forms for Thistle.

The Firhill club were then at the forefront of the game in Scotland, having just lifted the Scottish Cup by defeating Rangers 1-0 and finishing sixth in the First Division. They could boast names such as the veteran ex-Celt, Nap McMenemy and James Kinloch, who gave lengthy service as a player and director, and they also had current Scotland playmaker Jimmy McMullan in the side. McMullan in fact left Thistle as Gibson arrived but was soon to return and form a redoubtable partnership with the up-and-coming half-back, one that progressed to international level.

Crowds were exceptional at Firhill Park in those good old days. Over 49,000 saw a meeting with Rangers and attendances of 20,000 and 30,000 were the norm. Gibson claimed his place in the side for the 1922/23 season, operating at both right-half and centre-half with equal effect. At well over six feet, he was a handful in the air, and for such a tall, awkward-looking man he was dainty on his feet and was able to dribble as well as any forward. He regularly ended up in opponents' penalty areas and scored over 40 goals during his stay in Glasgow.

In the old, navy-blue colours of Thistle, Gibson developed strongly by playing alongside Joe Harris, another to earn international selection. Harris was soon poached by Middlesbrough but Jimmy McMullan returned to Firhill in 1923 to maintain a notable half-back line. It was the influence of McMullan that had much to do with Gibson's elevation to the international stage. A regular for the Scots since the First World War, McMullan pushed for the emerging half-back to be given an opportunity at national level whenever he could. In November 1925 Jimmy Gibson was picked for the Scottish League XI game against the Irish at Cliftonville. He knew a good display would probably see him on the short list for a full cap. The Scots won 7-3, and while Gibson didn't take the headlines – they were reserved for Hughie Gallacher who netted no fewer than five goals – Thistle's half-back slipped into his accomplished style easily. The selection committee were pleased with his performance and he was picked for the Scotland versus England meeting at Old Trafford, Manchester, the following April. McMullan was alongside his protégé and both played their part in a fine 1-0 victory.

Gibson had shown enough to become Scotland's first choice, with an added bonus that he was versatile enough to play in several positions, as an out-and-out playmaker or a stopper defender. He displaced his rivals and played in all of Scotland's three-match fixture list in 1926/27. Jimmy was quite brilliant in each match and was described as "a dominant figure on the field". His displays prompted a remarkable chase by English clubs to sign the leggy Scot.

Again Jimmy McMullan had a large influence on Gibson's future and on Thistle losing their star player. He had earlier moved to Manchester City and stories filtered back to Firhill of the high wages, good conditions and fringe benefits that could be secured in the Football League. Gibson decided he would move at the end of the season in search of a proverbial pot of English gold.

His father took control of negotiations as top clubs came in for him with almost open cheque books. He was the hottest property around. Manchester City, led by McMullan, chased him, as did Blackburn Rovers, Liverpool and Aston Villa. Everton were reported to be willing to offer as much as £10,000, far in excess of the 1925 record transfer fee of £6,550 for Bob Kelly. Huddersfield Town were also interested but it was Villa who became favourites although Jimmy knew little of it. Neilly Gibson put together a fabulous deal for his son, and by the time his father and Thistle officials were ready to finalise details they forgot to tell Jimmy which of the clamouring clubs he was joining! He didn't know which club he was signing for until just before the deal was concluded and he had to put signature to contract. Even at the last minute there was a bold assault by Huddersfield to tempt the player to Yorkshire. When on his way to Villa Park, Gibson was waylaid by Town representatives at St Enoch's station in Glasgow. But it was too late: he was by then an Aston Villa player. The fee . . . a new British record, £7,500 for the 26-year-old.

Brother, Willie Gibson, who lifted honours alongside Hughie Gallacher at Newcastle United.

Gibson arrived in the Midlands at a time of rebuilding at Villa Park following an era when the club were one of the giants of English football. After a season of settling into a different style of football, and different surroundings, Gibson was all set to help Aston Villa to honours in the coming 1928/29 season. His display at Wembley for Scotland in the magical 1928 match prompted Villa to be tipped for either the Championship or the Cup, such was the expectation of Gibson's influence. As it turned out, the Claret and Blues just missed out on both trophies, going down in the semi-final to Portsmouth and finishing third to Champions, Sheffield Wednesday. And Jimmy Gibson missed it all.

Luck deserted the Scot when he was badly injured, breaking a bone in his foot, and he played only five games all season, three of which were at centre-forward, showing again his versatility. His missing composure and constructive urge was undoubtedly a reason why Villa failed to win silverware.

With Gibson back in action, Villa again went close to the title the following year, ending fourth, and even closer in season 1930/31 when the Villa attack netted a record 128 goals by the end of the season. They were runners-up to Alex James's Arsenal, but had a delightful year nevertheless. Gibson was part of what is referred to as Villa's best ever half-back line, known as 'Wind, Sleet and Rain'. He partnered the sturdy Alec Talbot, another at over six feet, and English international Joe Tate, an outstanding tactician. They were the perfect middle line for an

Gibson in Aston Villa's ranks. Back row, left to right: *Gooch (trainer), Gibson, Smart, Jackson, Talbot, Tate, Moss.* Middle row: *Mandley, Astley, Brown, Walker, Houghton, Mort, York.* Front row: *Kingdon, Beresford, Blair, McLuckie.*

all-action forward combination led by Tom 'Pongo' Waring who grabbed 50 goals in that season. He was another England player as were Billy Walker, Villa's goalscoring skipper, outside-left Eric Houghton, another tremendous goalpoacher, and Joe Beresford, the stocky forager.

Gibson had a productive time in virtually every match feeding this dangerous line-up. It was football at its best. Goals came in abundance. Middlesbrough went down 8-1, Manchester United 7-0, Huddersfield Town 6-1, not only once but twice, and West Ham 6-1 too. Even Champions-elect Arsenal felt the Villa blast. They fell 5-1 during March in a marvellous exhibition by Gibson's side.

At the peak of his career, Gibson was another to sadly suffer from Anglo selection problems. His last two appearances for Scotland took place in 1929/30, and included a Gibson special . . . a 25-yard goal against Wales at Ninian Park. He was always noted for a thundering shot, but strangely never grabbed goals south as he did for Partick Thistle; there was no need due to Villa's glut of scoring forwards.

Gibson's Villa continued their frustrating sequence of being also-rans for the next three years, and this despite no shortage of adroit individuals on the Villa Park staff. In season 1931/32 they came fifth, in 1932/33 runners-up again. On that occasion Arsenal once more won the chase for the title trophy, but not before Jimmy Gibson had stamped his authority and versatility on an epic game in Birmingham on a cold November day in 1932.

The meeting of top and second clubs in the table attracted almost 60,000 to Villa Park. Only five players out of 22 on the pitch had not been capped and Gibson was, as one contemporary wrote, "striding, head and shoulders above everyone else in a game of footballing giants". He had a magnificent 90 minutes, reckoned to be his best for Villa. Operating as a defensive stopper, he showed how centre-halves could attack, a tactic maybe 40 years ahead of its time. He stormed upfield at every opportunity and smashed home an equaliser after the Gunners had taken the lead. In an absorbing contest Villa then went a goal up, only to be pegged back. Then Arsenal went in front again, only to see Villa once more equalise. Gibson in his defensive role subdued Alex James and David Jack, the men who made Arsenal tick, and Villa rallied to win the tussle 5-3. England schemer Jack said of the contest, "a game in which it was an honour to play and almost a pleasure to lose". The meeting was noted in Villa's annals as Jimmy Gibson's match.

The following year Aston Villa once more reached the semi-final of the FA Cup but caused a stir by going down to Manchester City by all of 6-1, just short of a record scoreline in the penultimate stage of the Cup. In that season Villa paraded no fewer than 15 internationals, mostly England men but alongside Gibson, Danny Blair, the ex-Clyde full-back and Joe Nibloe, signed from Kilmarnock, represented Scotland. However they just could not put their hands on a trophy.

Before Gibson's days as a pro footballer came to an end, he renewed acquaintance with Wizards' skipper, Jimmy McMullan, who had for so long during Gibson's early days had an influence on his career. The former Scotland captain was appointed Aston Villa manager at the end of that season, in May 1934. With the arrival of his ex-Partick Thistle mentor, Gibson, now past 30 years of age, could have expected a prosperous swansong. But McMullan was no sentimentalist. Villa struggled and Gibson, along with several other ageing stars, was axed. He played only nine games in the new season.

Gibson's decline, as happens to all stars, marked the end of a fine era at Villa Park, and also the deterioration of a great club which was not to rise again for many years in the future. The Claret and Blues had gone

Eric Houghton, one of Aston Villa's devastating forwards.

through a poor season but the very thought of relegation was unthinkable. Not only had Villa been League Champions six times, they had also taken the runners-up spot on eight occasions, as well as having lifted the FA Cup six times and reached another two finals. They were one of the élite of football with a hefty bank balance and purchasing power to attract big names . . . which they frequently did during this period.

But the impossible happened during Jimmy Gibson's final season, 1935/36. Villa's defence was no longer a powerful unit. Gone was the immense influence of 'Wind, Sleet and Rain', expensive replacements flopped and goals rushed into Villa's net from all angles. Manager McMullan departed and despite astronomical spending for the Thirties dreaded relegation quickly followed. They tumbled into Division Two for the first time in the club's distinguished history.

It was a sad end to Jimmy Gibson's days as a player in a career which had spanned 15 seasons. His final bow in football was against local rivals Wolves at Molineux in April 1936, one of several end-of-season do-or-die relegation confrontations. He retired in the close season and concentrated on a life out of football, becoming Industrial Labour officer at a Midlands ICI plant.

Gibson occasionally donned his gear for charity matches and even appeared for Villa once more, against Sutton Town in 1940. His was a

Jimmy Gibson, teamed up again with Jimmy McMullan at Villa Park.

classic talent long remembered by fans who lived through his generation. He seldom wasted the ball – was elegant even with his gangly legs which could stretch out to pull the ball down from almost impossible angles. Above all Gibson was able to operate in several areas of the field. For Villa he played in all half-back places, at inside-right and at centre-forward. He even ended up as goalkeeper in an astonishing match played in a snowstorm at St James Park, Newcastle. Villa lost by the ridiculous but highly entertaining scoreline of 7-5, but there was Gibson as adaptable as ever, between the posts when regular 'keeper Olney was led away injured.

Jimmy Gibson died aged 76 on New Year's Day 1978 at Erdington near West Bromwich in the heart of the Black Country. He had made a meagre eight appearances for his country, a figure that does no justice to one of the most competent footballers ever seen.

JAMES DAVIDSON GIBSON

Career Span: 1921 to 1936
Born: Larkhall, Lanarkshire, 12 June 1901
Died: Birmingham, 1 January 1978
Career: Kirkintilloch Rob Roy; Glasgow Ashfield; Partick Thistle, 1921; Aston Villa 1927; Retired 1936
Club Honours:
Football League Championship Runner-up, 1931, 1933
Scottish Junior Cup Runner-up, 1921
Full Internationals: Eight appearances, one goal, 1926-30
1925/26 v England
1926/27 v Wales, N Ireland, England
1927/28 v Wales, England
1929/30 v Wales (1), N Ireland
Scottish League XI: Two appearances, no goals, 1925-27
1925/26 v Irish League
1926/27 v Football League

MATCH ANALYSIS

Season	Club	League app-gls	Cup app-gls	Scotland app-gls	Other represent- ative app-gls	Total app-gls
1922-23	Partick Th. (Div 1)	22-8	*	—	—	22-8
1923-24	Partick Th. (Div 1)	30-9	*	—	—	30-9
1924-25	Partick Th. (Div 1)	30-6	*	—	—	30-6
1925-26	Partick Th. (Div 1)	34-6	*	1-0	1-0	36-6
1926-27	Partick Th. (Div 1)	28-11	*	3-0	1-0	32-11
1926-27	Aston Villa (Div 1)	1-0	0-0	—	—	1-0
1927-28	Aston Villa (Div 1)	24-1	0-0	2-0	—	26-1
1928-29	Aston Villa (Div 1)	5-2	0-0	—	—	5-2
1929-30	Aston Villa (Div 1)	26-1	3-0	2-1	—	31-2
1930-31	Aston Villa (Div 1)	39-2	2-0	—	—	41-2
1931-32	Aston Villa (Div 1)	34-1	3-0	—	—	37-1
1932-33	Aston Villa (Div 1)	38-3	3-0	—	—	41-3
1933-34	Aston Villa (Div 1)	27-0	1-0	—	—	28-0
1934-35	Aston Villa (Div 1)	9-0	0-0	—	—	9-0
1935-36	Aston Villa (Div 1)	10-0	0-0	—	—	10-0
Total		357-50	12-0	8-1	2-0	379-51

* Scottish Cup figures unknown.

7

TOM BRADSHAW . . . 'TINY' WAS HIS NAME

Few, finer players in the position . . . the complete contrast with the stopper.
Athletic News, 1928

DURING THE mid-Twenties followers of the game witnessed a feast of attacking, open football. Deadly, goal-mad centre-forwards were commonplace, tricky, penetrating wingers in every side, and subtle, graceful schemers a treat to watch. There were also plenty of big, cumbersome centre-halves, usually gruesome figures who handed out rough justice more often than not. But among the tree-trunk legs and massive shoulders, a few more cultured centre-halves took the field, men who had operated in the centre of midfield before an all-important change to the contentious offside law. Tom Bradshaw was one of that select group, a figure who could perform both roles, who could be tough and physical like many in that position, but who could also spread passes around the field in the style of a midfield maestro.

The alteration to football's rules in 1925 created dramatic changes in the way the game was played. The offside law was much the same both north and south of the Border, but it was the Scottish Football Association who proposed the change to Law 11 which had been in force since 1867. Up till then a player was offside if he was in the opponents' half of the field, in front of the ball and there were fewer than three players between him and the goal. Several defenders, notably Irish international Bill McCracken, worked an offside trap so well that football was becoming increasingly monotonous and unbearable to watch. Stoppages were frequent and all that could be heard was, "Offside! Offside!" on almost every attack, on every ground from Dundee to Southampton.

Football's authorities had to do something. In June 1925 they announced the offside law would be changed. A player now could not be caught offside if two opponents (instead of three) were nearer their own goal-line when the ball was last played. It was a huge success with a vast increase in goals and goalmouth action.

Prior to the alteration, team formation consisted of a goalkeeper and a defence of only two players — the full-backs — a midfield of three half-backs and five forwards. Now it was all change. To counter an increased danger from forwards who capitalised on added freedom up front, especially down the centre-forward track, players and directors

Tom Bradshaw, a strapping Scot from Bishopton.

– there were few managers then – came up with a tactical switch, moving the central midfielder, the centre-half of the old style, into a defensive role joining the full-backs. The stopper centre-half, or third back, evolved and the bigger and tougher they were, the better it was.

Tom Bradshaw, at six feet two inches and almost 14 stone, was a formidable frame of a man and fitted the new criteria perfectly. But Bradshaw, to coin a football phrase, could play a bit too. He was every bit as difficult for a forward to get past, dumping opposing Number 9s unceremoniously on the deck, but in essence Bradshaw always wanted to play football first and foremost, unlike a lot of his contemporaries during the inter-war years.

From Bishopton, Bradshaw made his name at unglamorous Gigg Lane, home of Bury Football Club, presently one of England's poor relations swamped by the Manchester and Liverpool giants. They are not a side usually associated with top-class international talent and their very name looks absurdly strange on the 1928 England v Scotland match programme. Yet in the Twenties, Bury went through their finest period in Division One, inspired by the commanding influence of the big Scot.

He had joined the Lancashire club following a glowing report from a Bury scout who had seen Bradshaw kicking a ball around in an unorganised scramble on a waste pitch in Glasgow. He had been playing for Coatbridge junior side, Woodside, in the North West Lanarkshire League and had already been spotted by one senior club, Hamilton. However after a trial, the Accies sent him packing back to the lower grade. It was to be a different story at Gigg Lane.

The Shakers gave the towering 18-year-old a month's examination in July 1922. Nicknamed 'Tiny' from school age, Bradshaw immediately impressed Bury's management. He performed well, was signed as a professional and pushed straight into the club's first XI, making his début in the opening weeks of the 1922/23 season. Bury were then in England's Second Division and he joined other young Scots from his own homelands, outside-right Davie Robbie from Motherwell and Hamilton left-half, Jimmy Porter. The three turned out regularly in the blue and white of Bury and had much to do with the club's days at the top in the coming years.

Before success of sorts arrived at Gigg Lane, Bradshaw and the Bury team went through an alarming few weeks during 1923 as a serious bribery scandal rocked the club. Bradshaw had nothing to do with the ignominy. In fact the incident related back to events in 1920 and a game against Coventry City. The sensational outcome was that the Shakers' directors and manager, William Cameron, were suspended by the Football Association and the club had to be completely remodelled. New boss James Thompson arrived and, as so often happens with an entire change in personnel, fortunes looked up for Bury.

In the following season of 1923/24, Tom Bradshaw emerged strongly, appearing in 31 League games, and Bury won promotion to the First Division. It was a return to the premier league for the first time since 1912 and it was achieved with a tense climax to the season. With all their fixtures completed Bury lay in second position to Leeds United, almost promoted but with the agony of waiting to see if one club, Derby County, could overtake them at the last moment. The Rams had one match left and were two points behind. Despite Derby winning convincingly 4-0, Bury still scraped home, by the tightest of margins – 0.015 of a goal!

Apart from Bradshaw, Robbie and Porter, three other notable players were in Bury's ranks. Up front Wally Amos and John Ball were a handful. Ball went on to represent England when at Gigg Lane, in the same year as Bradshaw was called up for Scotland. At centre-forward Norman Bulloch became something of a Bury legend. Also capped for England, he went on to appear over 500 times for the club and was later boss of the Shakers.

At 20 years of age Bradshaw's performance had been a revelation. One football critic noted his "clever footcraft and shrewd moves" as being "a delight to watch". In the First Division his reputation quickly

*Bury's line-up in 1928. Tom Bradshaw is pictured in the front row, third from the left.
England international Hugh Bulloch is to his left.*

spread even further as Bury went as close as they have ever done to winning the League Championship. On the opening day of the season, though, a record crowd of 33,523 at a virtually rebuilt Gigg Lane saw anything but a title-chasing team as they lost 2-0 to Manchester City. But after that Bradshaw's side went on to challenge high fliers Huddersfield Town, West Bromwich Albion and Bolton Wanderers. Bury fans had a real hope of seeing the trophy at their home base up to Easter, but then a dreadful sequence of results saw a slump to fifth position.

It was the same story in 1925/26 as Bury again challenged Huddersfield for the Championship. Again though they could not sustain the long season to the end, although they finished one place higher, in fourth spot, the best ever placing in the club's history. Bradshaw played in every game. Defensive partner Sam Wynne was another consistent performer for Bury and had a top-class understanding with Bradshaw at the back. Sadly Wynne became one of football's tragedies: he died during the course of a match with Sheffield United in April 1927. He collapsed after taking a free-kick and died in the dressing-room suffering from severe pneumonia. Football was shocked at the news, Bradshaw and his Bury team-mates stunned.

It was at this time that 'Tiny' was being talked about as one of the best centre-halves in the Football League. He had adapted perfectly to the new role after the offside law change, being strong in attack as well as in defence. His passes from the back were models of accuracy and he possessed the delicate touch, surprisingly so for such a massive pivot. Journalist Ivan Sharpe described him as "the complete contrast with the stopper". If he had a fault, it was his leisurely style and he was often prone to play intricate football to get out of trouble instead of thumping the ball with a hefty boot towards his forwards. Sharpe continued, "He was apt to overdo the constructive business by dallying with the ball in dangerous places." Once an infuriated Liverpool director said, "He is a wonderful player, but he will dribble the ball in front of his own goal. Once at least in every match he gives his directors a heart attack." Sharpe summed up though and noted that there were "few finer players in the position".

Like Tommy Law, and to a lesser extent, Jimmy Nelson, fans in Scotland had heard little of Tom Bradshaw. Bury, despite their fine showings, were not one of England's glamour clubs of the day and few reports on the Shakers filtered into Scotland. The national team's new offside system involved selectors in the dilemma of how to approach the advent of the defensive centre-half position. Once the law was revised the Scots fielded no fewer than 18 different players in the pivot's role in the years up to 1935. Nobody could say the shirt was his until Rangers defender James Simpson, father of goalkeeper Ronnie, stepped into action in 1934. Versatile half-backs like Dave Meiklejohn and Jimmy Gibson fitted into the position while good club men such as Allen Craig of Motherwell, St Mirren's George Walker and the McDougall brothers, James of Liverpool and Jock of Airdrie, were among defenders tried. Jimmy McDougall was later to be a colleague of Bradshaw's at Liverpool. Tom Bradshaw came into the reckoning in 1926 and 1927, a period which saw his side again reach a top-five place in Division One.

Bradshaw had come up against all the dangerous leaders England could find, strikers like Joe Bradford, George Camsell, 'Pongo' Waring, to name three of many, and also the best in the business, Everton's Billy Dean, Dixie to all. Tom impressed Scotland's eyes in the crowd and was given a chance to appear in front of a Scots audience in March 1928, in the Anglo-Scots v Home Scots contest. Bradshaw played himself into the national side with a composed performance. *The Bulletin* noted that he "never appeared to be stretched", and he also made the Anglos' goal in a 1-1 draw, hitting a precision pass for Tom Jennings to net.

It was a proud moment for 'Tiny' when the Scots line-up was announced a few days later. At 24 years of age, he replaced Meiklejohn and won his first cap in the game against England. Little did he know that it would be the only game he played for his country, in what is Scotland's finest performance in over 100 years of soccer.

On that afternoon at Wembley, Bradshaw, as one commentator wrote, "stood out like the Eiffel Tower". He was consistent and dominating for the full 90 minutes and mastered Dean in the year the powerful Number 9 just could not stop scoring. Tom Bradshaw would have

A move to Liverpool in 1930 – Bradshaw became the king-pin of the Anfield defence.

certainly won more honours for his country but for a nasty injury picked up in a League match as the new 1928/29 season got under way. He only appeared on ten occasions that year and missed much of the next campaign too. Scotland turned first to Queen's Park amateur, William King, and then to Meiklejohn again. Bradshaw was to remain, even when fit and playing for a good Liverpool side, the forgotten Wizard.

With Bradshaw's influence missing, Bury ended their brief love affair with Division One. They tumbled back into the Second Division and by the time the Scot was back to full fitness his days at Gigg Lane were limited. He was too good for the Second Division's rough-and-tumble and in January 1930 Liverpool paid out £8,250 for the strapping Number 5 who possessed such delicate skills.

Anfield in 1930 was, as it is now, a bastion of football. The Twenties had been good years for Liverpool. Twice Champions, they had fielded a string of noted players. The Thirties, however, did not

Berry Nieuwenhuys, one of Bradshaw's South African team-mates at Anfield. He was a most capable winger.

see a continuation of the glory days. The Reds finished in mediocre positions and even flirted with relegation on more than one occasion. They were to prove inconsistent but still had an array of talent on view.

Bradshaw formed a union in defence with two fellow Scots, Jimmy McDougall and Tom Morrison. Both were capped by Scotland and formed an international half-back line for the Reds. Morrison had been one of St Mirren's Cup-winning side in 1928 while McDougall made his name at Partick Thistle alongside Jimmy Gibson. Another international, Matt Busby, joined the line in years to follow. He was signed from Manchester City and would become a huge name in football.

In goal was a legendary character of the time, Ireland's Elisha Scott. England full-back Tom Cooper played next to Bradshaw, as did two well-remembered South African imports, Gordon Hodgson, scorer of 240 goals, and the slim and very effective left-winger, Berry Nieuwenhuys. A third Springbok, Arthur Riley, was also on Liverpool's books.

Bradshaw was appointed Liverpool's captain during much of his eight-year stay on Merseyside and went on to play almost 300 games, being observed as one of the club's best ever defenders. He took part in

THEY ARE LINING-UP FOR THE BIG KICK-OFF.

BIG TASKS START LEAGUE BALL ROLLING FOR EVERTON AND LIVERPOOL.

DEAN,
the Everton captain.

BRADSHAW
the Liverpool captain.

On Merseyside Tom was appointed Liverpool captain and had a great rivalry with his opposite number at Everton, Dixie Dean.

some amazing games during those years, including 7-4 and 6-0 victories over neighbours Everton. Liverpool lost 6-5 at Sunderland and even 9-2 on a New Year's Day holiday fixture at St James Park, Newcastle. The public certainly had their money's worth.

Season 1937/38 was to be Tiny's last at Anfield when, at 33 years old, he lost his place to Fred Rogers following two defeats in the opening weeks of the season, including a 6-1 reverse at Chelsea which spelt the end of the road for the centre-half. He remained with Liverpool for the rest of the football year but spent the time in Liverpool's reserve XI.

In September 1938, Bradshaw was approached by Third Lanark and he moved back to his native Clydeside for a small fee. At Cathkin Park, only a mighty goal-kick from hallowed Hampden, Bradshaw found himself playing in Scottish League football for the first time. Third Lanark had been Champions of the Second Division three years before and had established themselves in Division One. 1938/39 was to be a relegation struggle for the Warriors, though, and Bradshaw took little part in the battleground. He turned out in only five games and didn't relish Scottish football. In fact he returned quickly to Merseyside, signing up with Cheshire League side, South Liverpool, in February of that season, and remained in the area for the rest of his life. He worked for an insurance company based in Preston and later kept in touch with the game as a Norwich City scout.

'Tiny' Bradshaw lived to a grand age of 82, the oldest and last surviving member of the Wembley Wizards' line-up. He died in February 1986. Sir Matt Busby perhaps summed up Bradshaw aptly when he wrote, "despite his colossal build, Bradshaw was as dainty as an outsize pixie with the ball at his feet". That was Tom Bradshaw.

THOMAS BRADSHAW

Career Span: 1922 to 1939
Born: Bishopton, Renfrewshire, 7 February 1904
Died: 22 February 1986
Career: Woodside Juniors; Bury, 1922; Liverpool, 1930; Third Lanark, 1938; South Liverpool, 1939; later a Norwich City scout
Club Honours: Football League Division Two Promotion, 1924
Full Internationals: One appearance, no goals, 1928
1927/28 v England

MATCH ANALYSIS

Season	Club	League app-gls	Cup app-gls	Scotland app-gls	Other represent-ative app-gls	Total app-gls
1922-23 Bury (Div 2)		3-0	0-0	—	—	3-0
1923-24 Bury (Div 2)		31-1	1-0	—	—	32-1
1924-25 Bury (Div 1)		37-1	0-0	—	—	37-1
1925-26 Bury (Div 1)		42-2	2-0	—	—	44-2
1926-27 Bury (Div 1)		40-0	1-0	—	—	41-0
1927-28 Bury (Div 1)		40-4	4-0	1-0	—	45-4
1928-29 Bury (Div 1)		10-0	0-0	—	—	10-0
1929-30 Bury (Div 2)		5-0	0-0	—	—	5-0
1929-30 Liverpool (Div 1)		17-0	0-0	—	—	17-0
1930-31 Liverpool (Div 1)		35-0	1-0	—	—	36-0
1931-32 Liverpool (Div 1)		42-0	4-0	—	—	46-0
1932-33 Liverpool (Div 1)		39-3	1-0	—	—	40-3
1933-34 Liverpool (Div 1)		39-0	4-1	—	—	43-1
1934-35 Liverpool (Div 1)		31-0	2-0	—	—	33-0
1935-36 Liverpool (Div 1)		41-0	2-0	—	—	43-0
1936-37 Liverpool (Div 1)		31-0	0-0	—	—	31-0
1937-38 Liverpool (Div 1)		2-0	0-0	—	—	2-0
1938-39 Th. Lanark (Div 1)		5-0	0-0	—	—	5-0
Total		490-11	22-1	1-0	—	513-12

8

JIMMY McMULLAN . . . AN INSPIRING SKIPPER

A magician of a wing-half, who was an amazing passer of the ball and a superb tactician.

Sir Matt Busby, *Soccer at the Top*

SCOTLAND'S CAPTAIN in 1928 was a diminutive figure who never stood out in a crowd, yet on a football park was an outstanding midfield genius and influential skipper respected by all. Jimmy McMullan is one of a select group of footballers who can generally be regarded as one of Scotland's all-time greats, along with four other colleagues in that 1928 line-up; James, Jackson, Gallacher and Alan Morton. He had a long career in the game, both as player and manager, which included being involved in football through two world wars.

It was during the First World War that McMullan rose to prominence. The Wizards' captain was born in the town of Denny alongside the river Carron near Stirling. That was in March 1895, in an area noted for iron foundries and coal-pits, and he grew up as the industrial revolution transformed the country. McMullan played for a local club, Denny Hibernian and despite his lack of inches – he was only five feet five – proved a forceful player even at such an early stage in his career.

In 1912 Hibs reached non-League football's most prestigious final, the Scottish Junior Cup. At Firhill, home of Partick Thistle, they met Glasgow side Petershill and although McMullan's side lost heavily, by 5-0, it was an important day in the rise to fame of the pocket-sized half-back. Watching officials of Partick Thistle were impressed with McMullan's style and creative ability. They noted his name and kept a watch on his progress over the next few months. Thistle remained on his tracks and, although he was at Third Lanark for trials, they were the club to give the midfielder the opportunity of a professional footballer's life. Thistle signed McMullan in October 1913 when he was 18 years old.

The outbreak of hostilities on the Continent in the summer of 1914 was to restrict his development, but not as much as other young footballers of the era, especially those in England. South of the Border, the fighting eventually put a stop to normal soccer and regional leagues were organised with a very restricted set-up. Some top clubs, like Newcastle United and Sunderland, didn't even compete and closed down completely. In Scotland it was different, with football carrying on almost as if strife in Europe had never started.

JAMES McMULLAN
MANCHESTER CITY

Jimmy McMullan, one of Scotland's finest schemers.

When war broke out many people expected it would be over within a few months. In fact it was, of course, to last more than four years and by the time it was over more than 850,000 British servicemen would have been killed. Both ruling bodies in England and Scotland were under severe pressure to abandon the game. With such turmoil and suffering brought home to the public, playing a sport, especially for money, was quickly frowned upon. The Football League was cancelled but Scottish authorities gave their blessing to continue the League programme, although the Scottish Cup was suspended.

There was a huge debate in the press and strong reproach was levelled at Scottish football. The church, politicians, fans and players had their say. The *Glasgow Herald* commented, "The game is being gravely prejudiced and branded with a stigma." The Scottish League competition remained nevertheless, with fixtures regarded as official although it was announced that players should not be paid more than £1 per week and additionally they should all be engaged on war work. The Second Division was scrapped due to problems of travelling and availability of players. It was into this atmosphere that the young McMullan entered the senior grade . . . he went on to make quite a mark.

At Firhill, Partick Thistle did well in League football during those troubled years. They finished in a respectable position in each season,

Partick Thistle in 1921, the club's Cup-winning squad. Back row, left to right: *Lister (trainer), Hamilton, Crighton, Campbell, McMenemy, Wilson, Bowie, Borthwick.* Front row: *Johnston, Kinloch, Harris, Bullock, McMullan, McFarlane.* On ground: *Blair, Salisbury.*

as high as fourth in 1918/19. McMullan became a regular in the Jags' line-up, always coaxing and feeding his forwards. He was a cultured and inventive half-back who liked to keep the ball on the ground rather than provide a hopeful, skied 50-50 ball. With strong and powerful shoulders he was difficult to knock off the ball.

His commanding performances won him a place in Scotland's team for the Victory celebrations to mark the Armistice of November 1918. The four home nations played a series of games in the following Spring and McMullan played in all four of Scotland's fixtures. His début was against Ireland at Ibrox Park, but he almost missed the game due to travel problems in a country which was far from back to normal. Two players, McMullan and Alex McNair, were stranded at different railway stations on their way to the game. Scotland started with only nine men, McMullan arrived late to take his place, McNair didn't make it at all. Jimmy helped the Scots to a 2-1 victory nonetheless and went on to play well in the series, especially against England at Everton's Goodison Park, when the spoils were shared 2-2. He was also selected for the then important meeting between sides of the respective Leagues.

McMullan's first official cap for his country quickly followed as normal football returned . . . an international against Wales at Cardiff in February 1920. He replaced pre-war star Jimmy Hay and was

Jimmy became a Scotland regular and is pictured here in his country's side for the game against England in 1921. Back row, left to right: *Miller, Davidson, Ewart, Brewster, Blair.* Front row: *McNab, Cunningham, Marshall, Wilson, McMullan, Morton.*

Scotland's first choice at left-half for the next nine years, playing in all three games the following season as Scotland lifted the Home International Championship for the first time since 1910.

Partick Thistle continued their good form after the war period and in 1920/21 finished in sixth place and also won the Scottish Cup for the first time. Jimmy McMullan featured in Thistle's tough run to the final. They played no fewer than ten games to reach the last stage, including marathon contests with Hibs, Motherwell and Hearts. The Firhill club met Rangers in the final at Celtic Park, but had to face the Ibrox giants without the influential McMullan. He missed the game due to a kick on the ankle received in the Scotland versus England clash only days before. McMullan was immensely disappointed. Also missing from the Jags' finest moment was centre-half Willie Hamilton, another important player to the side.

Into McMullan's key role stepped veteran Jimmy McMenemy, Thistle's coach and very occasional player. But the underdogs rose to the occasion and won the Cup through a single goal scored by John Blair. McMullan was present and joined the celebrations afterwards. Thistle's party had a boisterous gathering in the unglamorous surroundings of the YMCA in Bothwell Street. The only displeasing feature of the day was the size of the crowd, only 28,294, one of the lowest ever for a

Scottish Cup final. Parkhead was a controversial venue to both 'Gers and Thistle fans, and with the entrance fee being doubled from one shilling to two shillings, something of a boycott took place in protest.

Shortly after all the Cup joy had settled down, McMullan was approached by agents of English clubs. Newcastle United wanted him and they offered £5,000, a massive fee, but Thistle turned down the offer without hesitation. They did not want to lose their strategist; however, McMullan was not happy. He was determined to play in the south and before the new season was underway had signed for an English club . . . not for Newcastle or for any of the top sides, not even for a Football League outfit, but amazingly for non-League Maidstone United in deepest Kent as player-manager.

It was a remarkable transfer. Non-League clubs in England had no wage restrictions so McMullan was to earn high money, but how and why a Scotland regular, one of the best in the Scottish League, disappeared to a grade of football fit only for old pros and rejects was perplexing to many. Certainly for Thistle. They received no transfer fee, a galling situation having turned down £5,000 only months before.

From Firhill, Jimmy went almost 500 miles to the south coast. It was an extreme change in landscape, from Glasgow's tenement blocks to the quiet villages in the Garden of England. The Scot immediately felt the effect of his move. He may have earned more in his wage packet but his name was removed from the national spotlight and he was dropped from the Scotland side, although he was still selected for the Anglo XI.

McMullan remained with the Stones for two seasons before returning to Partick Thistle almost as dramatically as he had left. In the close season of 1923 he was welcomed back to Firhill almost as a lost prodigal son. He was welcomed back by Scottish selectors too, being appointed as his country's skipper for the clash with England at Wembley at the end of the season. It was as if his unpopular sojourn in Kent had never happened.

Such was McMullan's talent. His special skills were in prime demand. Jimmy was a master tactician on the field and players relied on his leadership. He was a player of tenacious character, but not in a difficult unmanageable way, and above all he purveyed crisp, instant, accurate passes that almost snipped the top of the grass as they went.

That international with England was the very first at England's new home, Wembley. McMullan took over the captaincy from Jock Hutton and marshalled his side to a 1-1 draw. The captain's role during those inter-war years was given to several players; no one individual was given the honour for a prolonged period, unlike the modern era. Dave

McMullan, Scotland's playmaker, quit the first-class game in 1921 to join Maidstone United.

Morris took over for the next game and others, Tom Townsley and Willie McStay included, skippered the national side too. By the time Scotland were to return to Wembley four years later for an important date, McMullan would be in charge again.

As with many of Scotland's Wizards, and, for that matter, many

Back in the fold and captain of Scotland for the first international at Wembley in 1924.
McMullan joined Manchester City soon afterwards.

other stars in the game at that time, earnings caused much haggling in player-director meetings. Jimmy McMullan was well paid compared to others in his second spell at Partick Thistle. He received £7 per week, top wages because he was the special player. As Ian Archer wrote in his history, *The Jags*, McMullan was "the club's most outstanding player in a century". McMullan wasn't content though, he wanted more and pushed for better terms. They offered him £9 per week with a £2 win and £1 draw bonus, but it didn't satisfy the Scot and he demanded a transfer.

English football beckoned again for McMullan even though that the contract offered by his club was in fact more than the Football League maximum of £8 per week. This gave rise to speculation that special arrangements, perhaps illegal in the eyes of football's authorities, were rife in the south. Stories of hefty signing-on fees and under-the-counter payments, as well as additional jobs and rent-free houses being offered were commonplace. Jimmy was lured by this and severed his connection with Thistle for a second time.

Manchester City were the club that persuaded McMullan to try his luck in England again, this time in the big time. The date was 10 February 1926 and Thistle at least received a respectable transfer fee on this occasion – £4,700. Jimmy began a long and productive spell at Maine Road and in his first season saw both the heights and depths of top English soccer.

The intelligent, probing Scot was appointed captain of the Sky Blues. He joined City in the middle of a marvellous FA Cup run which ended up at the Empire Stadium. The Maine Road club had already defeated famous amateurs The Corinthians, League Champions Huddersfield Town, in front of 74,000, and Crystal Palace by the astonishing scoreline of 11-4 when McMullan entered the action in the sixth round. He faced a difficult trip to Clapton Orient in London. City were on target again though, winning 6-1 as McMullan combined with super-confident forwards Tom Johnson, Frank Roberts and Tommy Browell who banged home more goals. Local rivals Manchester United met City in a tension-packed semi-final at Bramall Lane, and it was McMullan who inspired the Sky Blues to a magnificent 3-0 victory over their deadly Old Trafford foes. Manchester was almost deserted with an exodus over the Pennines. One report noted City's performance as "a superlative display". City had netted a staggering 31 goals *en route* to the final.

Jimmy McMullan returned to Wembley where he had led out Scotland. This time he proudly marched out in front of King George V a City team which included full-back Phil McCloy, who had been in that Scotland side against England in 1924. City relied on their goalscoring aces again – Browell, Roberts and Johnson – as well as winger Billy Austin, who was able to net on a regular basis too. Both Frank Roberts and Tosh Johnson were England internationals, while Geordie, Tommy Browell, was most unlucky not to be recognised by his country. He netted over 250 goals in a sparkling career. Sam Cowan, England's centre-half, played alongside McCloy at the back. It was a side which in its day could demolish any team.

McMullan's eleven faced Bolton Wanderers, a club that was to play in three finals during the Twenties and win them all. City didn't perform to any sort of previous Cup form and fell to a 77th-minute strike by David Jack. City, in fact, put on a display at Wembley more suited to their League form which had in the latter half of the season been nothing short of a disaster.

The Maine Road club had gone through a change in manager in the season – McMullan was in fact signed by the directors – and eventually Peter Hodge, a Scot, took control, though not before City had slipped into the bottom placings of Division One. With the

Cup-final disappointment still in their minds, McMullan had to revive his team for a decisive relegation battle in the final games of the season. They did well at home to fellow strugglers Leeds United, winning 2-1, but then had to travel north to Tyneside in a last attempt to ensure First Division survival. The Maine Road outfit had to collect at least a point to stay up and in a truly dramatic climax to the season they lost 3-2, Austin missing an ever so crucial penalty. Ironically, McMullan's Scotland team-mate Hughie Gallacher did the damage; he grabbed a hat-trick for the Black'n'Whites. City were down despite having scored 89 goals – the most ever by a relegated club.

Within four months McMullan had gone through an eventful baptism in English football and his days at Maine Road were to continue in the same exciting vein. City just missed promotion in 1926/27, finishing third, and ended the season in dramatic fashion just as they had completed the previous campaign. They won convincingly 8-0 against Bradford City, as they had to, but rivals for the second promotion place, Portsmouth, won too and scraped into the First Division on goal average at City's expense. Had McMullan's side scored another goal and reached nine, they would have jumped straight back in what was one of the tightest Second Division races ever.

City, though, were to make no mistakes the next season. They walked away with the Championship and again their fans saw goals by the bagful. In McMullan's three seasons so far at Maine Road, his side had netted 110, 109 and 103 goals. The small and constructive schemer had much to do with this tremendous scoring prowess. 1927/28 had proved a momentous year in McMullan's career. Not only had he led Manchester City back to Division One in glorious style, he was recognised as the best left-half produced by Scotland since the war. Appointed national skipper again, he played a huge part in the Wizards' victory of that year both on and off the field. McMullan, now into his thirties, gave a marvellous display on the lush Wembley turf, prompting and sending his team forward with classic movements. Hughie Gallacher said his captain's performance was "the best as I have seen from any player any where". The *Glasgow Herald* noted that McMullan was "a master of strategy and judgement".

All told, McMullan appeared in 16 full internationals for Scotland, and in seven games against England was on the losing side only once. At the age of 34 he finally bowed out of the international scene in front of his own tartan masses, at Hampden Park in April 1929. Fittingly the Scots won 1-0 with a goal in the dying seconds. Jimmy was captain and 110,512 were there to see it.

Although the years were now catching up with McMullan and he was thinning on top, he was far from ready to bag his trusty football boots and call it a day. Jimmy played on until his 38th year, an automatic choice for Manchester City but for injury up to the end of the 1932/33 term, 21 seasons after his name had been noted by Partick Thistle directors in that Junior Cup final.

McMullan went out on a high note – back at Wembley, in another attempt to win a Cup medal. City had become a potent side, maintaining a deadly strikeforce as before. In season 1929/30 they finished in third place behind Champions Sheffield Wednesday, then in 1931/32 met Arsenal in the FA Cup semi-final, but went out to a freak last minute goal after outplaying the Gunners. The *Manchester Guardian* wrote after the shattering goal was scored, "McMullan stood dumbfounded like some great engineer whose life's masterpiece had been demolished by a paroxysm of nature."

Season 1932/33 was, as everyone said, to be McMullan's year . . . the finale of a marvellous career which had achieved much but never won any of the top medals, north or south of the Border. McMullan was the mainstay of the City side, despite ageing legs. He was now supported by a youngster from his old junior club Denny Hibs, a left-half who eventually replaced him in the City side, Matt Busby. The future Manchester United manager was to praise McMullan highly. The young Busby lodged in the McMullan household and Jimmy was like an uncle to him, looking after the youngster when days in the grimy but great city of Manchester became difficult. Busby said of the McMullan family, "They took me into their home and were one of the big reasons why I stayed in England at all." Busby was to model his own distinguished playing career on that of McMullan.

Jimmy switched to inside-left for much of the season and formed a great understanding with the unorthodox and fair-haired Eric Brook, England's match-winning left-winger. McMullan scored one of his rare goals as City thrashed Gateshead 9-0 in the third round of the Cup and embarked on their Wembley trail. Walsall, giant-killers of mighty Arsenal, fell, as did Bolton and Burnley. In the semi-final Derby County stood between the Mancunians and another final. At Huddersfield, in front of 51,961, the Rams were hot favourites but McMullan stamped his authoritative style on a game that swung from one end of the pitch to the other. The Scot set up City's second goal with a pass to Brook . . . a cross, and Fred Tilson, another of City's England strikers, headed home. Then in the 70th minute McMullan crowned a great afternoon with an imposing solo effort. Jimmy received the ball on the edge of the Derby penalty area and with typical expert control wriggled past two defenders as though he was a teenager, then waltzed round the 'keeper before shooting into an empty net. He was elated. The dream of ending his career with an FA Cup winners' medal was a distinct reality.

It was, however, not to be a fairytale ending for the ageing maestro. City faced longtime rivals Everton at Wembley and McMullan, for the third time, had a disappointing end to an epic Cup run. He had missed Thistle's victory, tasted defeat in 1926 and now, in 1933, was to be runner-up again. Everton cruised to victory by 3-0, with McMullan's Wizard colleague Jimmy Dunn scoring for the Goodison side. The occasion was too much for Jimmy McMullan: he was in tears at the final whistle, his dream ending sour. Dixie Dean, also in the Merseyside line-up, said, "My heart went out to him." It was a sorry sight watching McMullan troop away . . . and wearing the Number 13 jersey (it was the first final where players were numbered, from 1-22), a shirt which was distinctly unlucky. Matt Busby, who played in that game too, noted that the Sky Blues had lost the game in the dressing-room where nervous tension reached a peak, and City's players never recovered from what was pre-match agony.

Ironically Manchester City were back at Wembley within 12 months, and this time they won the FA Cup at last. But McMullan had by then retired. His final match was on 6 May 1933 against Huddersfield Town, a 1-0 defeat. Matt Busby said later of McMullan's ability, that he was "a magician of a left-half, who was an amazing passer of the ball and a superb tactician". He was short on inches but never short of enthusiasm or ideas.

Jimmy McMullan was the only member of Scotland's Wizards to enter the managerial side of the game. For such a quantity of talent it was surprising that no other player from the 11 immortals attempted what, even in the Thirties, was a jungle of intrigue and unexpected calls from the club chairman. Being the acclaimed tactician of both Scotland and Manchester City, Jimmy easily found a managerial post. Only a matter of days after hanging up his boots he was appointed boss of Second Division Oldham Athletic. He took over from another famed Scot, ex-Sheffield Wednesday centre-forward Andrew Wilson, at a time when the Latics were struggling at the wrong end of the table. McMullan's influence was instant, transforming a relegation outfit into one on the fringe of promotion within a season. Oldham's fortunes, though, were given a mighty jolt when Aston Villa enticed their new manager to the big-club set-up at Villa Park.

McMullan's reputation as a manager of abundant potential had pushed the Villa directorate into making a bold move to rid the club of antiquated practices. They cast away the old-style directors' committee which had run much of football for over 60 years and joined the rapidly

McMullan was the only Wizard to enter football management. Here he is pictured as boss of Aston Villa for the start of the 1935/36 season. Jimmy Gibson is third from the right in the back row. McMullan is seated in the middle row, extreme right.

changing world of the sport which saw team managers become almost as important as the star player. He became the Villa's first ever manager in May 1934, on a lucrative contract and in charge of a club recognised as one of the top three or four clubs in England. It was a huge step for the former Scotland captain, one which quickly became a traumatic experience.

Aston Villa were on the decline. They possessed ageing players, among them McMullan's international half-back partner, Jimmy Gibson. He had to rebuild and made a succession of big signings including Scottish caps Jimmy McLuckie from his old club, Manchester City, and Alex Massie, Jack Harkness's team-mate at Hearts. He spent a massive £35,000 on players but his new Villa side flopped, finishing 13th in 1934/35 and worse still in 1935/36. In that season the Claret and Blues were relegated for the first time in their history, a sensational event in the world of football during the Thirties. Changes were made week after week as McMullan attempted to stem the tide, but he never found the right blend. The season included a 7-1 hiding from Arsenal at Villa Park, the game in which Ted Drake had eight shots at goal and scored with seven of them! Inevitably Jimmy McMullan was held responsible for the intolerable failure. He was sacked as the proud club started life, embarrassingly, in Division Two.

It did not take the affronted manager long to get fixed up in a football post. As happens in soccer, managers jump on the merry-go-round and a' new job appears. McMullan found himself in charge of Notts County next. He was appointed the Magpies' boss in November 1936 and found an old Scots face there to welcome him – Hughie Gallacher, still playing and grabbing goals, although considerably older, slower and wiser.

McMullan discovered a perfect ally in Gallacher at Meadow Lane. The pair pushed the Division Three side up the table and County became favourites to regain their Second Division status. McMullan's tactical mind off the field and Gallacher's experience and goals on it proved a perfect match. County continued to be odds-on for promotion, leading the table until the closing weeks of the season. Success seemed well within their grasp but in the final run-in a crucial meeting with Brighton ended in defeat and Luton Town clinched the solitary promotion place, only one club from the lower divisions being promoted in that era. McMullan had lost out at the final post yet again but had boosted his flagging reputation as a manager following his unsuccessful spell in Birmingham.

Another top post came his way – the manager's chair of Sheffield Wednesday, and he moved to Hillsborough in December 1937. But McMullan joined the Owls when they were in a desperate position. They had just been relegated from Division One and were firmly rooted at the bottom of the Second Division. However, from the opening days of the new year McMullan inspired Wednesday and with an average of a point a game they scrambled clear of a second successive slump.

The momentum was carried on into the new season. The Owls made a strong bid for promotion as the Second World War approached. However Jimmy McMullan's club career, whether as player or as manager, was always fated to collapse at the last hurdle. It happened again as Sheffield United, of all teams, leaped over their Yorkshire rivals and went up by a single point. McMullan had done a good job in revitalising the Hillsborough club, however. He wasn't a tough disciplinarian – in fact Jimmy was criticised in some quarters for not being hard or aggressive with players. He preferred the gentlemanly approach, asking players to do things his way, rather than demanding. It worked only in part.

There was much optimism that Wednesday would be successful in the 1939/40 season, but Adolf Hitler's swift advance across Europe put an end to such thoughts. War, in an even more devastating manner, stopped McMullan's managerial progress in a career that never started up again once the fighting had ceased.

He remained part-time boss of Sheffield Wednesday for the early years of the war, while he also took a job in a local factory helping the war effort. The Owls struggled under difficult circumstances, like many clubs in wartime football, and in the spring of 1942 his contract was not renewed. Wednesday's vice-chairman made the comment, "We've not fallen out with Jimmy but feel our decision is in the best interests of everyone in the present circumstances." It was a blow to McMullan, the end of his career in the game. He said, "If there had been no war I should have remained with Wednesday for many years." He had formed a good side, one containing astute signings and several talented young players. The war ruined a promising career. The Scot said, "I have become one of the victims."

Afterwards Jimmy left the game that he had served so well for 30 years. He had been unrivalled at left-half for a decade, unsurpassed as a link-man and such an encouragement to others. He resided in Sheffield, a factory worker until his retirement. Jimmy died in 1964 when 70 years old.

JAMES McMULLAN

Career Span: 1913 to 1942
Born: Denny, Stirlingshire, 26 March 1895
Died: Sheffield, 28 November 1964
Career: Denny Hibs; Partick Thistle, 1913; Maidstone United, 1921; Partick Thistle, 1923; Manchester City, 1926; Oldham Athletic manager, 1933; Aston Villa manager, 1934; Notts County manager, 1936; Sheffield Wednesday manager, 1937 to 1942
Club Honours:
Football League Division Two Champions, 1928
FA Cup runner-up, 1926, 1933
Scottish Junior Cup runner-up, 1912
Full Internationals: 16 appearances, no goals, 1920-29
1919/20 v Wales
1920/21 v Wales, Ireland, England
1923/24 v N Ireland, England
1924/25 v England
1925/26 v Wales, England
1926/27 v Wales, England
1927/28 v Wales, England
1928/29 v Wales, N Ireland, England
Victory Internationals: Four appearances, no goals, 1918-19
1918/19 v England, England, Ireland, Ireland
Scottish League XI: Four appearances, no goals, 1919-21
1918/19 v Football League
1919/20 v Irish League
1920/21 v Irish League, Football League

MATCH ANALYSIS

Season	Club	League app-gls	Cup app-gls	Scotland app-gls	Other represent- ative app-gls	Total app-gls
1913-14 Partick Th. (Div 1)		20-0	*	—	—	20-0
1914-15 Partick Th. (Div 1)		*	*	—	—	*
1915-16 Partick Th. (Div 1)		*	*	—	—	*
1916-17 Partick Th. (Div 1)		*	*	—	—	*
1917-18 Partick Th. (Div 1)		*	*	—	—	*
1918-19 Partick Th. (Div 1)		26-1	*	—	5-0	31-1
1919-20 Partick Th. (Div 1)		26-2	*	1-0	1-0	28-2
1920-21 Partick Th. (Div 1)		29-2	*	3-0	2-0	34-2
1921-22 Maidstone Utd		*	*	—	—	*
1922-23 Maidstone Utd		*	*	—	—	*
1923-24 Partick Th. (Div 1)		26-2	*	2-0	—	28-2
1924-25 Partick Th. (Div 1)		29-2	*	1-0	—	30-2
1925-26 Partick Th. (Div 1)		23-0	*	1-0	—	24-0
1925-26 Manchester C. (Div 1)		10-0	3-0	1-0	—	14-0
1926-27 Manchester C. (Div 2)		35-3	1-0	2-0	—	38-3
1927-28 Manchester C. (Div 2)		38-4	3-0	2-0	—	43-4
1928-29 Manchester C. (Div 1)		38-0	1-0	3-0	—	42-0
1929-30 Manchester C. (Div 1)		25-2	3-0	—	—	28-2
1930-31 Manchester C. (Div 1)		27-0	—	—	—	27-0
1931-32 Manchester C. (Div 1)		21-1	5-0	—	—	26-1
1932-33 Manchester C. (Div 1)		26-0	6-2	—	—	32-2
Total		399-19	22-2	16-0	8-0	445-21

* League/Cup figures unknown.

9

ALEC JACKSON . . . THE GAY CAVALIER

I am in football because I like the game, but also to make my living, and as all men I want the most I can get from the job.

Alec Jackson, August 1932

DURING THE close season break of 1932 the football world was spellbound with a much publicised dispute at Chelsea Football Club. Three Wembley Wizards were at the centre of a summer of discontent at Stamford Bridge; Tommy Law, Hughie Gallacher and Alec Jackson. It was Jackson who made all the headlines though, pursuing a bold stand against the maximum wage rule, an irritating source of restlessness among stars. At the time he was one of the game's foremost attractions, a flamboyant character with a film star profile, the best right-winger in the business . . . the best there had ever been, many claimed.

He was tall, a graceful, gazelle-like mover with the ball, able to cut in from the touchline and score from most positions more than any other in his role. He possessed dash, flair and the touch of genius to turn a game. One description of the day noted, "A more dynamic and attractive player never donned a pair of football boots." Yet at only 27 years of age, at the peak of a distinguished career, he turned his back on senior football, disillusioned with the professional system. He left the first-class game in search of bigger financial rewards. Alec Jackson caused a sensation like few before.

Imagine the uproar and controversy if one of the current game's superstar players, perhaps Mo Johnston or Ian Rush, was forced to earn, say, £100 per week as a maximum wage instead of several thousand pounds. Imagine the headlines when they refused, made a stand over earnings and quit the League for a minor club like Linlithgow Rose or Colne Dynamos. It would be a story that would fill sports pages with intrigue for months. Back in 1932 it happened. The superstar was Alec Jackson and the clubs involved were fashionable Chelsea of the First Division and Cheshire non-League outfit Ashton National.

Chelsea's set-up at the time was in a sorry state of affairs, known in some quarters as "the school of scandal and correction". Throughout the 1931/32 season there had been grumblings about money, bonus payments and fringe benefits. Chelsea's stars, the Wizards' plus other internationals like Alex Cheyne and Andy Wilson, were at the forefront of a bid to obtain a better deal than the £8 per week maximum wage, and they had a point. There was a huge disparity between footballers at

Alec Jackson, a flamboyant character on the right wing.

the top of their profession and other sportsmen. They believed strongly that players should be paid like all artists, according to their drawing power. Chelsea put thousands of pounds into their coffers through the turnstiles and why should the likes of Jackson and company not take a share? Other sports personalities of the era earned much more. Tennis stars like Fred Perry or Rene Lacoste received thousands, while golfers and boxers took home as much. In the United States, baseball stars were getting £10,000 per year and cricketers too were on more money than top footballers. England's best batsmen and bowlers, such as Hobbs, Sutcliffe and Hammond, received up to £15 per match. Even in association football itself, managers could obtain sizeable rewards. Both Herbert Chapman of Arsenal and Peter McWilliam of Middlesbrough were reported to be earning as much as £2,000 per annum. Yet the nation's star players were restricted to around £500 per year. It was a poor man's sport.

Alec Jackson was urged on by lucrative contracts being offered by continental sides. French clubs in particular were frequently in London in search of talent, and staggering sums were being talked about. Jackson thought he could win a fight to obtain more. Although Gallacher and Law backed the principle they made peace with Chelsea's officials. Jackson did not. He saw Andy Wilson and Alec Cheyne depart for France, signing for Nîmes. He could have joined them but decided to struggle on with his battle against authority. He refused to believe that a man of his absolute capabilities could be disregarded. He was wrong. Football clubs had the upper hand every time in the Twenties and Thirties, unlike now when

a order
naps he
come to

back waiting
..o, last season
United, Gates-
st.

Peter House, who has return.
manage Leicester City, has memor.
the success of Scots at Filbert-street.
has made up his mind to allow Scotsmen
to bring back the past glories of the
City.

..irren and :
the thunder o
Celtic. Will t

MAN OF THE MOMENT.

'on

Ru

ball

Englar

r.

ALEX JACKSON

THE "FREE LANCE" FOOTBALLER.

ALEX Jackson, famous Scottish
international, scorer of match-
winning goals in League and Cup
and representative engagements, is
out of League football, setting a
new fashion by declaring himself a
free lance professional footballer.

What does the term mean and what
effect will this departure have on the
future of professionalism? When it was
announced a few weeks ago that Alec,
so frequently referred to as an Aber-
donian, though really a son of
Dumbartonshire, had signed for Ashton
National, it was a bombshell indeed.

The Scot will be a "free lance,"
because his agreement with the Cheshire
League club covers a month only, and
at the end of that time the contract may
be renewed or terminate.

Will Ashton National gain by their
strange adventure? Probably, for the
name of the Cheshire League club will
be almost as much in the public mouth
as that of Arsenal, at least till the
novelty of the situation wears off. The
inclusion of Jackson in their ranks will
be a draw for the time being.

It is all very intriguing and, quite
naturally, other players of established
reputations, with ideas of their own
about the fixing of a maximum wage
beyond which the brightest stars of the
day cannot legitimately go while in the
service of a League club, will follow the
course of events very keenly.

ENGLAND'S
coming Rug
will hinge largel
of the selectors
duce a successo
who was the las
backs seen in F
England's gre:
was at half-back
Spong and Sobe
were tried against
and Elliott (Uni
Gadney (Leiceste
the matches with
In neither inst
succeed, and a g
fast and resourc
were often forced
It was the wea
Calcutta match th
so distinctive a s
were barely entit.

AVENUE

It has to be adm
changes in the Se
duced new ideas
explore avenues I
general scheme of
The Midlands
were searched.
T. W. Brown, t
was revived again.
R. A. Gerrard G
(Gloucester), amo
C. Webb (Dev
G. Gregory (Br
successes of the y

COUNT

County teams
strength of their
The Northern (
strengthened by
of Durham, who
ing depression v
ship without en
Cheshire, wit'
ran second to I
Cestrians' effort
The Northern
when the inter:
review,
Northumberl
forward in J
Northern (New
all the interna
other player t
was J. P. M
Lancashire 'hi
Scotland in t
The North
some leeway
of players
selectors of

matter
The

South-
A good
omotion
and the
Taylor,

Valuable,
yers of
ounders
in the
valiant
season
nat the
an last

l time
o even
team.
higher
ans to

be in
play-
ttles
land-

be
most
rlisle

season.
and it
o fewer
o even

balanced
erience.
i clever
l. and
defence

quan-
young
If he
evens
ints

ing
ap

Starting With A R:

By

LANCASTRIAN.

In
you
sta

*Headlines in the Evening Express in August 1932. An intriguing story that kept
newspaper men busy.*

in many instances stars rule and clubs obey. Jackson was perhaps half a century before his time.

Chelsea Football Club's official comment was, "The directors are sick and tired of the whole business . . . there is no room at Chelsea for dissatisfied players, even internationals." The Londoners placed Jackson on the transfer list at a ludicrously low fee of £4,500, almost half of what they had paid for him, but attracted no offers. Despite his undoubted footballing talents his reputation as a troublemaker went against him. In August 1932 he stunned the football world by declaring himself "The Freelance Footballer", quitting Football League soccer and moving outside the jurisdiction of the League and Football Association's archaic and repressive rules. It was to the non-League arena that Jackson's unique freestyle, unorthodox, wing play went – to the impressive sounding Ashton National Club, in reality a backwater of football in the suburbs of Manchester.

He fixed up his own wages on a monthly contract with extra payments based upon his drawing power at the turnstile. As Jackson said, "it was gate appeal", just as, 50 years later, Kevin Keegan had negotiated with Newcastle United. He also observed at the time, "I shall play four home matches for a sum far greater than a League club could pay. I am in football because I like the game, but also to make my living, and as all men, I want the most I can get from the job."

Jackson aimed to pick up as much as four times his Chelsea weekly wage. He was guaranteed £15 per week and ten per cent of gate receipts. He was hoping to earn almost £40 per week, big money in 1932.

The eyes of football were on the Scot's insidious but gallant adventure. The game's top performers, the likes of Gallacher and James included, were watching eagerly. If Jackson succeeded then there would be a flurry of names wanting to follow his lead. The maximum-wage rule would come under severe pressure.

Ashton National had to be congratulated on their enterprise in securing Jackson. Their name hit the headlines alongside Arsenal and Rangers for the first and only time, albeit for a few short weeks. Ashton's chairman likened the signing to cricket, where some of the sport's most noted personalities played outside the first-class game – as they do even today. Learie Constantine, the West Indian Test star, was appearing for Nelson in Lancashire League cricket in the Thirties.

Ashton had met Jackson at the Dorchester Hotel and fixed up the deal that, as their chairman hoped, would, "have its reward in the form of bumper gates". The Cheshire club possessed a ground that could hold up to 20,000 and attracted gates in the region of 5,000 for visits from such grandiose opposition as Winsford, Nantwich and Macclesfield, who eventually won the League in that 1932/33 season. Jackson's début was not a happy one though. A healthy crowd turned up, but Ashton lost 2-0 to Northwich Victoria, and the former Scottish international found it difficult to adapt to a game that saw the ball in the air more often than not, with Jackson receiving few accurate passes. He commented in the *Liverpool Evening Express*, "I'm more disappointed than I can say." The standard of football was far from what he was used to.

Despite having other noted ex-professionals in their line-up, including another Scottish forward, Duncan Lindsay, whose claim to fame was that in one match he had scored six goals for Cowdenbeath, Ashton's season was not the massive success Jackson hoped for. Attendances were never of the quantity required to finance such an inventive deal and the club quickly got into cash problems. Alec, though, as forthright as ever, tore up his lucrative contract to help the club out.

In February 1933 he joined another ambitious non-League side, Margate, but again his "Freelance Footballer" philosophy did not work. In 1934 Jackson almost moved out of football and around several lesser clubs including Streatham Town, eventually ending up in France with a spell at Nice on the Mediterranean coast. No doubt a few contented faces were to be seen in the Chelsea boardroom. Chelsea had lost massively on the Jackson saga. His games for the club had cost over £100 per match and the Cockneys recouped not one penny of their near record £8,500 outlay.

Yet the way one of football's greatest ever players drifted from view was something of a tragedy, mirrored in many ways by George Best, two generations later. But Alec Jackson had left countless memories of his wonderful match-winning ability in stays with Aberdeen, Huddersfield Town and Chelsea. He always appeared to enjoy the game, hence the nickname 'The Gay Cavalier'.

Jackson was born on the edge of Loch Lomond, in Renton, in 1905, the son of a tinsmith. It is a town with no real football connections nowadays, but in Edwardian Scotland it was a community with a famous link with the origins of football in the country. The old Renton club were even declared Champions of the World in 1888! He was christened Alexander Skinner Jackson, the youngest of five brothers, several of whom also entered football. Walter signed for Kilmarnock and John emigrated to the States where he helped introduce soccer to the land of baseball.

Alec attended school in nearby Dumbarton and started playing football in serious competition with juvenile side Renton Victoria. When 16 years old he was good enough to be asked for trials with League club Dumbarton, another pioneer side north of the Border. He was taken on at Boghead Park and signed professional in 1922 at a time when the club was relegated from the Scottish First Division.

Even at such a young age Jackson played with supreme confidence, a quality which never deserted him. It was said that he even boasted that one day he would play for Scotland – true or not, it was soon to happen. The lithe, almost skinny, teenager did well in the black and gold hoops of Dumbarton, but just when he was establishing his name, he decided to quit Scottish football and join his brother's club in the USA. Off Jackson sailed, to Pennsylvania where he joined Bethlehem Star for the 1923/24 season. Alec's other brother, Walter, went with him, both lured by profitable contracts. Financial reward was always near the top of Alec's priorities, even at such a young age.

The skyscrapers and open spaces of America didn't really suit the Jacksons, however, and when Jock Hume, an exiled former Aberdeen full-back with New York's Brooklyn Wanderers, spotted the pair, he sent reports back to Pittodrie raving about a young strip of a lad called Alec Jackson. Aberdeen boss Paddy Travers was interested and wanted Alec, although he didn't really require his brother. However, in the summer of 1924 they paid less than £1,000 to get them both as Alec wouldn't accept a move unless his elder brother was purchased too. The deal was concluded in the Caledonian Hotel in the Granite City. Alec was back in Scotland, and in Division One, back in black and gold colours too, this time the stripes of the Dons.

Aberdeen put the roaming forward – he was never merely to stick to a yard of touchline like many wingers – straight into the first-team against Rangers. On his second appearance at Ayr, Jackson crashed home his first goal, while his brother Walter, at centre-forward, got the other two in a 3-3 draw. In fact Aberdeen's first 11 goals in the 1924/25 season were all netted by the Jackson family.

Aberdeen had quite an attraction to the name of Jackson that year. Apart from the Jackson brothers they also fielded half-back Jimmy Jackson, who hailed from Newcastle, and then signed Willie Jackson, "Stonewall" as he was to be known. He was from Renton, like Alec, but was no relation.

Alec Jackson's rise to fame was rapid. He consistently turned out brilliant performances on the Scottish League circuit and won rave comments. And this when in a struggling Don's side which only scraped away from bottom place on the last day of the season. Alec had done so well that he was picked for Scotland in the meeting against Wales in February 1925 when aged only 19 years 278 days. One of the youngest ever débutants for the Blues, he went on to play in all three internationals that year.

Against the Welsh at Tynecastle, Scotland fielded almost a complete Wizards' forward line. Only Alex James was missing. Scotland won 3-1 and they were on top in their next match as well, winning comfortably again, 3-0 over Ireland. In April, Jackson lined up against England in a Scots team that had been picked entirely from home-based players. They won once more, by 2-0, and the young Jackson was declared man-of-the-match and was presented with the ball as a memento. In front of 92,000 at Hampden Park he faced Sam Wadsworth, a highly experienced full-back, yet the England man never got near the new Scotland wonder. Jackson was so quick and with that speed, allied with excellent close control, he proved a handful. Alec was dubbed "The Flying Scotsman" by the press, while his Aberdeen boss referred to him as a "human greyhound".

Clearly Aberdeen could not hold on to the emerging talent for long. English clubs had been alerted after his performance at Hampden Park and Jackson was soon to head south. He had been at Pittodrie for only a season but had made a huge impression. English football during the Twenties belonged largely to one club, Huddersfield Town, and it was fitting that Jackson's immaculate skills should end up among the trophies at Leeds Road.

Huddersfield were a team facing bankruptcy and complete dissolution as the decade opened, but, remarkably, turned their near disaster into triumph. They won promotion and reached the Cup final in 1920, lifted the Cup in 1922, were third in the Championship a year later, then won the coveted title in both 1924 and 1925. And that wasn't the end of their glory now Jackson was added to their squad.

Led by the eminent Herbert Chapman, perhaps the greatest manager of all time and certainly a pioneer among football bosses, Huddersfield paid £5,000 for Jackson. It was one of Chapman's last acts before joining Arsenal and he couldn't have left the Leeds Road outfit a better parting bequest. It was the portly manager's negotiation technique that persuaded Jackson to join Huddersfield rather than one of a glut of clubs chasing the Scot.

Jackson spent five happy years in Yorkshire and his pace and opportunism made an immediate impact on English football. He was perfectly suited to Huddersfield's set-up and with the offside law change, Town's array of forwards were too potent to stop. Billy Smith, to oppose Jackson for England at Wembley in 1928, held the other flank. George Brown was an England centre-forward and grabbed 35 goals in Jackson's first season. G.W. Cook chipped in with 14 goals while Alec himself got 16. Clem Stephenson at inside-forward made the line work. He was another international and the third Geordie in the front line.

They opened the 1925/26 season with a great run of ten games without defeat and, in a race with Arsenal and Sunderland, won the League Championship with two games to spare. On the eve of the General Strike, Huddersfield Town wrote their name into soccer history, the first side to win three League titles in succession. It was Alec Jackson who all but

The Jackson brothers, Alec and Walter, in Aberdeen's side in 1924. Back row, left to right: *Edwards, Jackson (J.), Blackwell, Forsyth, Davidson, Hutton.* Front row: *Jackson (Alec), Cosgrove, Jackson (Walter), Paton, Smith.*

clinched the record, netting twice against West Ham on Easter Saturday, goals which made certain Arsenal could not catch them.

After continuing to help Scotland to some commanding victories, 3-0 and 4-0 over Wales and Ireland, Jackson finished off the season in style. He scored the only goal of the England versus Scotland clash at Old Trafford, combining with Gallacher in a delightful piece of teamwork before firing the ball in off the post and into the net. It was the climax to a marvellous season for a lad who was still barely 21 years of age.

The treble Championship holders almost made it four in a row the following season. Jackson was joined by Bob Kelly, another star forward, and formed a right-wing duo to match the Stephenson-Smith combination on the left touchline. It was Hughie Gallacher's Newcastle United that robbed Alec of another title medal and the Terriers had to be content with runners-up spot.

In season 1927/28, a year when his club narrowly missed securing the double, Alec Jackson reached his peak. He earned acclaim as "one of the greatest outside-rights who ever played football" after scoring a hat-trick for the Wembley Wizards against England. Much was written about the five-foot ten-inch-tall, sleek outside-right. He had a soft Highland voice, sparkling eyes and always a grin. Jackson was a handsome and wonderful personality with charisma which captivated all fans, whether sporting blue and white favours or not. Colleague Hughie Gallacher later wrote, "In my view he was a complete winger, above all he had the ability to cut in and score a goal when it was needed." Jackson netted over 130 goals in his career, many by racing in from his by-line to meet crosses from the opposite wing . . . just as he did at Wembley in 1928. It was an exceptional total for a winger.

Hudderfield's double challenge reached an astonishing climax at the end of the season when they played several crucial matches in a fortnight, including a semi-final replay, the FA Cup final, title deciders and, for five of the side, a certain England versus Scotland meeting too. It was a hectic and thrilling period but in the end it was too much of an ordeal. Yet despite losing all, official Huddersfield annals still suggested "that this was the most memorable season in the club's history".

Alec Jackson played a big part, scoring 24 goals. In the FA Cup Huddersfield demolished all opposition in earlier ties; Middlesbrough 4-0, Lincoln City 4-2 and Tottenham 6-1, a game when Town's forwards hit magical heights. Relegation strugglers Sheffield United faced Huddersfield in a semi-final which developed into a marathon watched by 192,369 spectators. At Old Trafford the game ended 2-2, then at Goodison a goal-less replay followed. On 2 April they met once more, at Maine Road, and, a matter of two days after his glory at Wembley for Scotland, Jackson was back creating the news of the day. He ran in from his wing to send a second-half header into the United net for the only goal of the game.

Jackson returned to the Empire Stadium and Huddersfield were the hottest favourites for years. They faced Blackburn Rovers, 100-1 outsiders, a club threatened with the drop into Division Two. Yet in an extraordinary final, Blackburn won convincingly against all the odds. Rovers went 2-0 ahead with two soft goals while Jackson and Smith never got the service required until well into the match. When they did Huddersfield looked dangerous. The *Sunday Times* noted one Jackson run "With the ball at his toe, he went half the length of the field and passed at least four men." His trickery on that occasion came to nothing; however, with a liking for the unique Wembley atmosphere, the Scot fired on all cylinders again. He put his team back into the game when he fastened on to a pass and hit a strong shot that ricocheted into the net off the 'keeper and via the bar. Rovers were not to be caught though. They scored again the Cup went to Lancashire.

The dream of a League and Cup double was over but Huddersfield were still favourites for the Championship. In the backlog of fixtures that followed, though, only four points resulted and Everton crept home ahead of Jackson's side. It was a season waged with an almost unchanged line-up. Apart from the brilliance of the international forward line, Huddersfield also fielded Goodhall, Wilson and Wadsworth, all England men. The side's personalities were known everywhere, their images on the cigarette cards which were collected in those days by thousands from all age-groups and all areas of the country.

A move to Huddersfield Town took Alec into the English First Division and to much success. Back row, left to right: *Redfern, Goodall, Mercer, Wilson, Brown, Steele.* Front row: *Jackson, Kelly, Stephenson, Smith, Barkas.*

Alec Jackson was never far from creating news. Huddersfield, although slipping up in League competition in 1928/29, continued to do well in Cup football and they reached the semi-final stage again. But it was on the international front, in Belfast, that Jackson made more headlines along with his great buddy, Hughie Gallacher. Scotland scored seven goals against the Irish and the game was noted as "the Gallacher and Jackson show", Alec grabbing two goals, creating three others and Gallacher netting five.

At Hampden Park, Jackson was the centre of attention once more. In a physical encounter with the Auld Enemy, Alec was tackled heavily just before half-time by Ernie Blenkinsop, England's full-back. He fell badly and cried out with pain from a broken arm and collar-bone injury. Jackson was carried from the field and taken to the nearby Victoria Infirmary along Battlefield Road. Although sedated with chloroform and half-dazed he was suddenly aroused by a mighty roar from the 110,512 crowd . . . the Hampden Roar. Alec Cheyne had just scored the decider in the dying minutes. Jackson called out, "Nurse, nurse! That's the winning goal for Scotland." He then resumed unconsciousness with a satisfied smile on his face.

The following year was to be Jackson's last in Huddersfield's blue and white. It proved to be another exciting season, the fifth in succession at

Jackson quickly became an instant hit south of the Border, featured in a set of cigarette cards by Mac'.

Leeds Road. The Terriers were back in Cup mood and Jackson led the trail to another Wembley appointment, scoring nine of Town's 11 goals. He had a particular relish for the magic of the FA Cup. Alec netted 23 goals all told in only 36 ties. Bury, Sheffield United and Bradford City were eliminated, then Aston Villa in a tough confrontation. They met Sheffield Wednesday in the semi-final and it was Jackson who hogged the show. At Old Trafford in front of 69,292 fans he found the net twice to give his club a 2-1 victory and this after Mark Hooper had put Wednesday in front in another all-Yorkshire semi-final. Jackson pounced on the stroke of half-time with an equaliser. Billy Smith crossed, an Owl's defender handled and knocked the ball on to Jackson who hesitated, expecting a certain penalty. But after an extraordinary few seconds when everyone stood still for the referee's decision, Jackson reacted first when the whistle didn't go and lashed the ball into the net. In the second half the Scot grabbed his second with a superlative effort. From a corner he side-stepped Blenkinsop, his full-back rival at Hampden Park, and fired in a left-foot shot which bulged the netting once more.

118

A big transfer to Chelsea saw Alec play alongside fellow Wizards Gallacher and Law, together with a host of other Scots.

Former boss at Leeds Road, Herbert Chapman, the man who signed Jackson, led his Arsenal side against Huddersfield in the final. The Gunners were just starting to react to Chapman's winning touch and a great match was in store. It was the side who dominated the Twenties against the team to win almost everything in the Thirties. Alec Jackson had to take a secondary role in the showpiece, though, his fellow Wembley Wizard in Arsenal's ranks, Alex James, seeing the Highbury club to a fine 2-0 win.

It was the last major game Jackson played for Huddersfield. He also appeared for the last time for Scotland too, against France, his 17th appearance. He was another to be caught in the Anglos' disagreement. Jackson scored eight goals for the Scots and only once played in a losing team.

Although he started the new 1930/31 season in Huddersfield's colours and in splendour, he was quickly to join Chelsea in a blaze of publicity. The Londoners had just been promoted back to Division One and had substantial cash resources to spend. They had already splashed out on

Gallacher and Cheyne, and Jackson was their next target. They saw the winger play in an unaccustomed centre-forward's role and register a stunning hat-trick against Manchester United as the season got underway. Chelsea officials took out their cheque book – Alec Jackson was to head for Stamford Bridge.

The confidential fee was rumoured to be as high as £12,000, a new record, although many sources published a lower figure of £8,500. He was more than happy to move to London where Chelsea's set-up was known as "The Scottish Regiment". They offered him top money and several fringe benefits came his way. He was one of the first footballers to lend his name to advertisements and, for a fee of £5 a time, Alec appeared in the sports department of a prestigious London store. Jackson also received payment, together with a complimentary shave and hair cut thrown in, for visiting a fashionable hairdressing salon, and he also took over a public-house in the West End in St Martin's Lane. He became one of the highest paid men in English football, living in sumptuous surroundings in Shepperton alongside the Thames.

Alec made his début at Stamford Bridge against Sheffield Wednesday and grabbed his first goal three games later in a 4-0 win over Middlesbrough. Chelsea had a good opening season and the following year Jackson reached yet another FA Cup semi-final, scoring 16 goals from the wing. London suited his cavalier approach to life, he was able to swagger around trendy districts of the metropolis and relished a rivalry with Gallacher, and with Alec James at Arsenal, as to who would be regarded as the top sportsman of the capital.

The dressing-room atmosphere at Stamford Bridge, though, was to quickly turn into a hornets' nest of trouble. Chelsea's management could be criticised for not being able to handle their superstars, but the stars themselves were the main cause of unrest, especially Gallacher and Jackson, two tempestuous Scots characters. Gallacher recorded in his life story that they were very close – "we had a lot in common", he noted.

Jackson, for all his great football skills, was a happy-go-lucky personality, a joker who loved to live life to the full. He was, too, vain and argumentative, much like Gallacher. The centre-forward recorded one incident in Chelsea's dressing-room which indicated the deteriorating relationships between players at Chelsea. Jackson always knew he was one of the best and played on the fact at every opportunity. He once entered the changing-room and said to a lesser colleague "Fancy me, the Great Jackson, getting the same pay as you!" Arguments raged and a lot of pushing and pointing took place. Stamford Bridge became a centre of derision, not of football. It all resulted in Jackson's sensational, if unnecessary, exit from football.

Alec Jackson. Sadly, he was killed in a road accident when aged only 41.

Following Alec's unsuccessful foray into non-League circles and then French soccer, Jackson returned to London where he became a popular licensee in the years up to World War Two. He was a partner in the Queen's Hotel at Leicester Square where he retained his bubbling nature behind the bar.

He entered the army during the war and served in the Middle East, playing football in regimental matches which always saw a number of famous ex-pro's entertaining the troops. He was elevated to the rank of major, a welfare officer – Jackson's personality being ideally suited to mixing with the rank and file. Sadly Jackson never returned home. In 1946, soon after the war had ended, he was driving a three-ton lorry along the dusty Suez canal road near Cairo. The lorry was involved in an accident in which it skidded and overturned, and Jackson was badly injured. He died in hospital shortly afterwards.

Alec Jackson was only 41 years of age. It was a tragic ending to a man who was an immense box-office attraction, a player who could mesmerise and confound opponents, delight spectators and, alas, irritate football's hierarchy. John Rafferty wrote in the Scottish Football Association's centenary history, that Jackson was a player, with "laughter in his eyes and magic in his feet".

ALEXANDER SKINNER JACKSON

Career Span: 1922 to 1932
Born: Renton, Dunbartonshire, 12 May 1905
Died: Cairo, Egypt, 15 November 1946
Career: Renton Victoria, Dumbarton, 1922; Bethlehem Star, 1923; Aberdeen, 1924; Huddersfield Town, 1925; Chelsea, 1930; Ashton National, 1932; Margate, 1933; Nice, 1934; Retired, 1938
Club Honours:
Football League Champions, 1926
Football League runners-up, 1927, 1928
FA Cup runner-up, 1928, 1930
Full Internationals: 17 appearances, eight goals, 1925-30
1924/25 v Wales, N Ireland, England
1925/26 v Wales, N Ireland, England (1)
1926/27 v Wales (2), N Ireland
1927/28 v Wales, England (3)
1928/29 v Wales, N Ireland (2), England
1929/30 v Wales, N Ireland, England, France

MATCH ANALYSIS

Season	Club	League app-gls	Cup app-gls	Scotland app-gls	Other represent-ative app-gls	Total app-gls
1922-23	Dumbarton (Div 2)	25-2	1-0	—	—	26-2
1923-24	Dumbarton (Div 2)	2-0	—	—	—	2-0
1923-24	Bethlehem Star	—	—	—	—	—
1924-25	Aberdeen (Div 1)	34-8	6-0	3-0	—	43-8
1925-26	Hudd'sfield (Div 1)	39-16	2-0	3-1	—	44-17
1926-27	Hudd'sfield (Div 1)	32-6	1-0	2-2	—	35-8
1927-28	Hudd'sfield (Div 1)	39-19	8-5	2-3	—	49-27
1928-29	Hudd'sfield (Div 1)	35-14	6-5	3-2	—	44-21
1929-30	Hudd'sfield (Div 1)	30-8	7-9	4-0	—	41-17
1930-31	Hudd'sfield (Div 1)	4-7	0-0	—	—	4-7
1930-31	Chelsea (Div 1)	29-10	5-3	—	—	34-13
1931-32	Chelsea (Div 1)	36-15	7-1	—	—	43-16
Total		305-105	43-23	17-8	—	365-136

10

JIMMY DUNN . . . THE JOKER IN THE PACK

His wonderful runs and well directed passes made him a menace.
Daily Express, 1932

SCOTLAND'S TEAM of 1928 contained several players who liked a bit of fun, more so than a normal football XI. Gallacher, James and Jackson were three mischievous grown-ups, but above all little Jimmy Dunn was the jester-in-chief, a joker in the pack. Dixie Dean, for long a close friend and team-mate of Dunn's at Everton, noted, "He was always contriving some practical joke to play."

Colleagues of Dunn's, whether with Hibernian, Everton or Scotland, were always fearful of being a victim of his sense of humour. He would get up to all sorts of tricks and pranks, and in the most nerve-racking of moments. Even before the FA Cup final of 1933 he couldn't resist the urge to cause hilarity. Everton's side had been nicely rigged out in matching suits, shoes, hats and coats, all made to measure. Jimmy Dunn was up to his pranks though. When no one was looking he nipped into the dressing-room and mixed up all the sizes so that when each of his team-mates tried on their spanking new outfit they looked, as Dean remarked in his biography, "like extras from a Mack Sennet comedy".

There was another incident, at a top hotel, when Dunn sneakily pinned a pair of his discarded breakfast kippers to the underside of the dining-room table, walked away and left them. A day or so later new guests and hotel staff were perplexed as to where a putrid smell that had engulfed the hotel was coming from!

At five feet six inches tall with curly auburn hair and a cheeky Scots manner, he could easily have become a music-hall comic. He even possessed a remarkable resemblance to latter-day comedian Charlie Drake. As it was, Jimmy Dunn was an expert footballer, who was not only hugely gifted with the ball, but was also noted for ceaseless effort over 90 minutes. He was bubbling with energy and enthusiasm.

Dunn was another Wembley Wizard who hailed from Glasgow and its surrounds. In fact only Jimmy McMullan, from Stirling, came from another part of Scotland. Dunn attended school in Govan and played football for the soccer nursery of St Anthony's. He was capped at junior level, was noticed by Hibernian and for all of £20 signed for the Edinburgh club during the summer of 1920.

Davy Gordon was in charge of the Easter Road team in days when Britain was patching itself together after a horrific four-year war. He

Jimmy Dunn, a titch of a man from Glasgow.

was soon to make way for Alex Maley, but the former Hull City player threw the young and feeble-looking Dunn into the Scottish League against Airdrie along with another raw recruit, goalkeeper Willie Harper. Despite a defeat at Easter Road, 1 September 1920 was a significant date for Hibs fans, for both players went on to establish themselves as Scotland players. Other names quickly to become stars in Edinburgh entered the action too, Walker, Halligan and Harry Ritchie included.

Season 1920/21 was not one of Hibernian's better seasons. By autumn they were down to 15th in the table, but gradually the team settled and climbed into the top five, eventually finishing in seventh place. Jimmy McColl arrived to wear the centre-forward shirt and the team which was to contest two Cup finals in a row had all but come together. Dunn had progressed well, being selected for the Scottish League side in October 1922 along with colleagues Harper and Ritchie.

Hibs' performance in the Scottish Cup up to 1923 had been a disaster. In 1920 they fell to Armadale, the following year to Partick Thistle, and in 1922 to Motherwell, all in early stages of the competition. By the time the first round tie of 1923 against Clackmannan was due to be played, the Hibee faithful were anything but confident. Hibs though, were now a different side, evolving into a strong unit. Jimmy Dunn made the inside-right berth his own with displays of hard work and craftsmanship that defied his frail appearance. He was tricky and could wallop a fierce shot at goal.

Hibernian's Cup run in 1923 featured seven games and Dunn played well in all. They had the luck of home draws, not once having to leave Easter Road except when they reached the semi-final. Even a replay with Peebles Rovers was played in Edinburgh. Hibs were on form, not losing a goal, defeating Clackmannan, Peebles, Queen's Park and Aberdeen, helped by a first-minute goal from Dunn. They faced Third Lanark in the semi-final and Hibs still held ground advantage, the tie being played in the capital, albeit at Tynecastle. Dunn steered his side to the final, grabbing the only goal of the semi after Third's goalkeeper, Muir, dropped the ball. The wee man pounced in a flash and Hibs were at Hampden Park.

Celtic versus Hibernian was an eagerly anticipated match, the battle of the greens – and a grim, defensive contest it turned out to be. There was little time or space for Dunn's craft in a close match watched by 80,100 spectators. A blunder by Willie Harper, who had been a secure last line of defence in the games up to the final, gave the Cup to Celtic. He misjudged a cross during the second-half and allowed Joe Cassidy to score the only goal of the game. Hibs had been unlucky considering their opening pressure and superiority.

Jimmy was, however, to get another chance of a Cup medal 12 months later. Hibs returned to the final to meet Airdrie with exactly the same line-up, thought to be a unique achievement. Harper was in goal – by then the ex-Scots Guardsman and heavyweight champion had been called up by Scotland. Willie McGinnigle and Willie Dornan operated at full-back to complete the defence. Willie Miller was at centre-half with the experienced Peter Kerr an automatic choice at right-half. Hugh Shaw, of massive build, was on his left. Up-front ex-Celtic star McColl led the line and was the side's chief goal-getter. Dunn ably supported him in grabbing goals, totalling over 100 for Hibs during his stay at Easter Road. Johnny Halligan formed a left-wing partnership with Darkie Walker, while 13-stone Harry Ritchie was on the right flank, a Hibs terracing favourite.

Hibernian reached the final after a gruelling Cup excursion unlike their 1923 run. They struggled to dispose of the then Alliance side, Dundee United, and took two matches to fell Alloa. Up against League Champions, Alan Morton's Rangers in round three, Hibs came back from being a goal behind to win 2-1. An epic victory was seen by 52,885 and described by *The Scotsman* as "a sensational achievement". Three games followed against Partick Thistle, then another three in a marathon effort in the semi-final with Aberdeen. It took Hibs a minute short of five hours to defeat the Dons.

Airdrie fielded a powerful XI during the mid-Twenties, with Hughie Gallacher and Bob McPhail among an efficient side. At Ibrox, scene of the final, Jimmy Dunn again had an unhappy afternoon as the Diamonds ran out 2-0 winners. Jimmy in fact should not have played. He had turned out even though unfit, but as Hibs' most important link-man he couldn't be missed. Early into the game Dunn felt his injury and had to retire, becoming a virtual passenger on the wing.

In season 1924/25 Jimmy almost made up for his Cup final disappointments and had a marvellous year. Hibs challenged for League honours and Dunn crashed home 25 goals, the top scorer and a more than useful return for an inside-forward. A settled line-up continued and Hibs, after being leaders in March, finished in third place behind Champions Rangers.

Dunn had missed a medal yet again but he was rewarded for an impressive season with Scottish caps against, firstly, Wales and then Northern Ireland. He made his first appearance alongside another débutant, Alec Jackson, while in the 3-1 victory over Wales, Hughie Gallacher got his first scoring efforts for Scotland. It was a sign of things to come from an exciting forward line. Against the Irish the tenacious Dunn also scored his first goal for his country, sent away by Gallacher in the 35th minute to score with much glee.

Jimmy Dunn was by now Hibs' most valuable asset. He was leading scorer again in 1925/26 but the club's fine XI which had gone so close to ultimate victory was now breaking up. The Hibees were still one of Scotland's strongest outfits, though, and came close yet again to Cup victory before Dunn departed south for Merseyside.

In the 1928 tournament they were handed a walkover against Dykehead who scratched, then took care of Third Lanark, Falkirk and Dunfermline before meeting up with Rangers once more in the semi-final. Hibs had beaten the Ibrox men the week before but, with a neutral venue, unusually at Hearts' ground again, the Blues romped to a 3-0 win. Dunn, along with right-wing partner Harry Ritchie, played for Scotland that year. Willie Robb was a third member of the Hibs side to be capped.

The slight figure of Hibs' inside-forward had passed a century of goals for his club that season and was well respected in Scotland if hardly known south of the Border. His performance as one of the Wizards in 1928, though, pushed his name into the spotlight of English clubs and his days in Scotland became severely numbered.

Dunn had secured his place in the Scots line-up with a bit of fortune. Against Ireland he was only one of the short list of reserves but when Alex James cried off because of club commitments, along with other

English-based men, Jackson, McMullan and Gibson, Dunn stepped into a reshuffled side. He partnered Ritchie on the wing again and, despite a 1-0 reverse for the Scots, Jimmy performed so well, including netting a disallowed "goal" due to handball, that he was pencilled in for the selectors' team for the next international, suitably against the Auld Enemy. The Hibs forward saw off rivals Sandy Russell, ex-Airdrie and then with Preston, Bob McKay at Newcastle, and the veteran maestro of Ibrox, Andy Cunningham.

The Scots' right-wing triangle at Wembley of Dunn, Gibson and Jackson completely dominated the English trio. Jimmy Dunn had Healless chasing his diminutive figure all afternoon and the Scotsman's tremendous work-rate was in complete contrast to the style of Alex James on the left side of the field. They forged a balanced middle line for the Scotland team.

Apart from Alan Morton and Jack Harkness, Dunn was the only other member of the side who played his football in Scotland. After Wembley it was only a matter of weeks before he too moved to one of the big arenas of England. Football League champions, Everton, one of the richest clubs in the country, were on his trail. The Goodison Park club rushed in with a bid for Dunn almost immediately after the Wembley international. On 20 April 1928, 'Ginger', as he was known, signed for the Mersey club. Everton made a double swoop on Easter Road, taking Jimmy's colleague, Harry Ritchie too.

The Hibernian pair teamed up with Dixie Dean, fresh from his record 60-goal burst, for the start of the 1928/29 season. The new forward line made their début at Bolton. They clicked – Everton won and Dean netted a hat-trick. But after a satisfying start the English champions slumped amazingly. Everton finished in relegation trouble, 18th in the table, and the following season was even worse with the club dropping into Division Two for the first time in their history.

Several players had lost form including both Dunn and Ritchie. Jimmy lost his confidence and his place in the side while Ritchie quickly returned to Scotland, to Dundee. It seemed Jimmy Dunn's taste of English football had turned sour – but out of the mire ascended a new Everton side, one to take England by storm.

Football is celebrated for dramatic changes in fortune and so it happened at Goodison Park. After such a catastrophe – there could not have been worse than Second Division football – three wonderful years of success followed and Dunn was back in favour, very much a part of Everton's set-up. The Toffees accomplished the rare achievement of winning promotion, then the Championship and following on to FA Cup victory, all in successive seasons.

Everton put together a goal-hungry front combination with Dean the

Dunn pictured in Hibernian colours. Back row, left to right: *McGinnigle, Ritchie, Harper, Pempleton, Miller.* Front row: *Murray, Duncan, Dunn, Kerr, McColl, Walker.*

ultimate threat, and Dunn, his chief confederate. Fellow Scot Jimmy Stein was at outside-left, Tosh Johnson, with McMullan at Maine Road, a cunning inside partner, and the rousing Ted Critchley on Dunn's right flank. They swept through the Second Division scoring goals in an unprecedented way. On one occasion against Charlton all five forwards netted within the space of 17 minutes. By December they had scored 55 goals and by the end of the programme had netted no fewer than 121 goals, an average of three a game. They won Division Two's trophy by seven points. Dean grabbed 39 of those goals while Dunn backed him up with 14. The *Daily Express* noted Dunn's contribution to Everton's side: "His wonderful runs and well directed passes made him a menace." He had pace to leave defenders rooted to the spot and accuracy in finding corners of the net.

Everton were within a whisker of reaching the FA Cup final that year too. They lost by a single goal to promotion rivals West Bromwich Albion in the semi-final after a convincing journey through the rounds. Disappointment was quickly forgotten though as the Merseysiders rattled all First Division opposition they encountered in the following season. It was Dunn who got them off to a flying start with a super hat-trick in the opening game of the season against Birmingham City. They headed the table by October and in some quarters were described

Jimmy in action for Everton following his big transfer after the Wizards' match.

as "invincible". They were assured of the title before the season's end and, although Dunn missed a chunk of the programme through injury, he was back for the run-in, making a welcome return in a 5-1 victory over Sheffield United, a game in which he netted two goals.

Now over 30 years old, 'Ginger' continued to pick up injuries which caused him to miss several games, but he was a regular in Everton's FA Cup success of 1933, winning a marvellous treble of medals which made up for the frustrations at Easter Road. Everton reached the semi-final stage, knocking out Leicester City, Bury, Leeds United and Luton Town, all in convincing style. At Molineux, lowly Second Division West Ham United stood between Dunn and Wembley Stadium. In a game that Everton should not have won, Jimmy was one of the few Mersey men to play to form. He put the Blues ahead, then saw the Hammers equalise before creating the winner for Ted Critchley.

Little Jimmy Dunn was an important link in Everton's side, here caricatured after his side had defeated Aston Villa 4-2 during the title chase of 1931/32.

In the final he opposed the Wizards' captain in midfield, Jimmy McMullan, veteran of opposition Manchester City. Dunn was apprehensive about returning to Wembley for the first time since 1928 and facing a near 100,000 crowd. He complained of an ankle strain before travelling to London, but as Dixie Dean recalled, the centre-forward had the ideal solution to Dunn's so-called injury: "I knew that it was nothing more than nerves he naturally felt and suggested to the directors that Dunn be told the club would choose Johnnie McGourty as there was a doubt about his fitness." As soon as the little Scot heard he might be left out, he was miraculously fit and raring to go.

Everton swept to FA Cup glory, winning 3-0. Stein scored the first and Dean the second, while Jimmy Dunn registered number three . . . a goal he knew little about. Ten minutes from the end his curly

Everton's FA Cup-winning squad of 1933. Back row, left to right: *Cook (trainer), White, Britton, Sagar, Thompson, Cresswell, Cook.* Front row: *Critchley, Geldard, Dunn, Dean, Johnson, Stein.*

head went for a Geldhard corner with several City defenders. He was left prostrate in the penalty area, almost unconscious. A few seconds later he heard roars from the Everton end of the stadium and saw blurred colleagues pulling him up with huge smiles. His header had found the back of the net ... Dunn realised he had scored and started a merry jig reserved for those special moments of Cup glory.

Apart from Everton's star forwards there were several other players who achieved considerable stature in the game. Nine full internationals were included in the line-up. Warney Cresswell was a dour Tynesider and capable full-back while Cliff Britton and Ted Sagar were also household names. Albert Geldhard, who first played senior football when only 15 years old, was on the wing and Billy Cook partnered Cresswell at the back. He had won a Scottish Cup medal with Celtic two years earlier and wing-half Jock Thomson had faced Dunn many times in the Scottish League when at Dundee.

Age caught up with Jimmy Dunn quickly after that Cup party. But before his days on Merseyside were over two amusing incidents which centred around the Scots joker occurred, marvellously recorded by Dixie Dean. The pair were great friends, room-mates in the Everton camp. They looked a strange couple too, five-foot six-inch Dunn of slight build, Dean at six feet with massive shoulders. Nevertheless, they were rarely parted.

On a club tour to Germany during the early Thirties, Everton's party experienced the Nazi doctrine that was gathering pace. Although Dunn and his colleagues refused to give the Nazi salute in Dresden in front of the likes of Hermann Göring, they later had a brush with the new regime's tough police. In Cologne several of Everton's players were relaxing in a hotel lounge when a German rogue picked on the smallest of the group – Jimmy Dunn. He was robbed and the little Scot chased after the thief. German police were called and while the robber got away, Jimmy was arrested, to the astonishment of his Everton colleagues. Dunn, with typical Scots anger, caused such a commotion he was dragged off towards the police station, but the giant Dean went to his rescue. The England centre-forward pleaded with the police but was getting nowhere fast. Events were getting out of hand and very ugly when Dean grabbed a Nazi policeman and shouted to Dunn, "Run for it, Jimmy," and the Scot fled down the strasse, arms and legs pumping like a 100-yard sprinter. Dean meanwhile had knocked out one of the opposition and was set upon by another. He woke up next morning in a police cell, bruised and battered! Everton's chairman eventually had the not-too-easy task of sorting the incident out and restoring diplomatic relations. Dunn wasn't charged but Dean was fined and ended up with several broken fingers, the result of a splendid punch fit for the boxing-ring.

The little and large duo of Dunn and Dean were involved in another incident when the club sailed for the Canary Islands on another end-of-season tour, this time in 1934. The pair were billeted together as usual and did anything but enjoy their stay in the sun. One evening they were caught up in a disturbance when returning to their hotel in Tenerife. A rattle of gunfire was too close for comfort and on top of the perpetual British problem of coming to terms with the heat and the variety of strange insect life, they had suffered enough. It was back home as quickly as possible. They jumped on board a banana boat, the *Dunbar Castle*, heading for England and leaving the rest of the Everton squad behind!

Jimmy Dunn lost his place in Everton's side during February 1934 and appeared only sparsely for the Blues after that. He was almost 35 years old when Exeter City purchased his Scottish talents in May 1935. Jimmy found life difficult in the Third Division South. From the very top of the game he sampled life at the very bottom. The Grecians had a terrible season propping up the whole Football League and having to apply for re-election at the end of the programme.

Within 12 months Merseyside beckoned a return in the shape of Runcorn, and Dunn was appointed player-coach during the close season of 1936. Jimmy's days in the limelight were now over but to his utmost pleasure the name of Dunn was not lost to the footballing public. He had three sons, all of whom played soccer, one to reach the top just like his father and to win an FA Cup medal too.

James Dunn Junior developed into a fine goalscoring inside-forward from teenage days as a Liverpool and England boys' player. He joined Wolves and was part of the Wanderers' victorious Cup side in 1949 that defeated Leicester City. He later also turned out for Derby County.

Jimmy Dunn was a wonderful footballer, able to combine ball skills, hard endeavour and goal awareness. He was also a bubbly, jovial character, the life and soul of the dressing-room. Sadly, he died of cancer in 1963 when 62 years old.

JAMES DUNN

Career Span: 1920 to 1936
Born: Glasgow, 25 November 1900
Died: 20 August 1963
Career: St Anthony's, Hibernian, 1920; Everton, 1928; Exeter City, 1935; Runcorn player-coach, 1936; Retired, *c.*1939
Club Honours:
Football League Champions, 1932
Football League Division Two Champions, 1931
FA Cup winner, 1933
Scottish Cup runner-up, 1923, 1924
Full Internationals: Six appearances, two goals, 1925-29
1924/25 v Wales, N Ireland (1)
1926/27 v N Ireland
1927/28 v N Ireland, England
1928/29 v Wales (1)
Scottish League XI: One appearance, no goals, 1923
1922/23 v Irish League
Scottish Junior International: One appearance, 1920

MATCH ANALYSIS

Season	Club	League app-gls	Cup app-gls	Scotland app-gls	Other represent- ative app-gls	Total app-gls
1920-21	Hibernian (Div 1)	34-11	5-1	—	—	39-12
1921-22	Hibernian (Div 1)	38-6	2-2	—	—	40-8
1922-23	Hibernian (Div 1)	35-7	7-3	—	1-0	43-10
1923-24	Hibernian (Div 1)	30-7	11-4	—	—	41-11
1924-25	Hibernian (Div 1)	35-25	1-0	2-1	—	38-26
1925-26	Hibernian (Div 1)	36-15	3-0	—	—	39-15
1926-27	Hibernian (Div 1)	33-10	1-0	1-0	—	35-10
1927-28	Hibernian (Div 1)	27-8	5-2	2-0	—	34-10
1928-29	Everton (Div 1)	24-4	1-0	1-1	—	26-5
1929-30	Everton (Div 1)	12-0	1-0	—	—	13-0
1930-31	Everton (Div 2)	28-14	5-3	—	—	33-17
1931-32	Everton (Div 1)	22-10	0-0	—	—	22-10
1932-33	Everton (Div 1)	25-10	6-4	—	—	31-14
1933-34	Everton (Div 1)	23-4	1-0	—	—	24-4
1934-35	Everton (Div 1)	6-0	0-0	—	—	6-0
1935-36	Exeter (Div 3)	21-4	0-0	—	—	21-4
Total		429-135	49-19	6-2	1-0	485-156

11

HUGHIE GALLACHER . . . OF THE MAGIC FEET

Players like Hughie Gallacher appear only once in a generation.
Tommy Lawton, ex-England centre-forward

IF THERE ever was a footballer destined to become a newspaper man's dream come true, then Hughie Gallacher was that player. From his early days as a teenager, through the Twenties and Thirties when he was a household name, to a tragic finale, Gallacher created news, be it with scintillating skills on the football field or controversial moments off it. No matter what he did, Gallacher made the headlines.

There have been few players who have made such an impression on the game of football. At five feet five inches tall, he was a rough, tough little centre-forward, something of a loveable rascal. He was equipped with a complete range of skills few have equalled. To many who saw his footballing repertoire he was the best Number 9 of all time, better than Dean, Lofthouse, McGrory, or any other exalted centre-forward over the years. Some may have been bigger and more forceful but none had the quite brilliant all round ability of Gallacher. England's Raich Carter said, "there has never been better", while Tommy Lawton made the comment recently, "If he was around today, then I don't think £2 million would buy him. Players like Hughie Gallacher appear only once in a generation."

Gallacher was the most talked about player during the years between the two wars. He was the biggest headline maker of the era, creating sensation, controversy and intrigue wherever he went during a 20-year stint in the game: headlines like the day he represented the Scottish League in 1925 which typified his career, in the spotlight on the pitch and off it.

Gallacher was in Belfast for a League select contest with the Irish, a game in which he totally destroyed the home XI with a devastating display. He netted five of Scotland's goals in a 7-3 victory. It was a Scottish record and all of Hughie's goals were netted in succession, three inside 14 minutes. Not only had the diminutive Lanarkshire forward regularly found the net, but he also made the Irish players and watching fans feel distinctly second-rate with irritating, teasing tricks on the ball, taunting the opposition almost to a frenzy.

At half-time a note was passed into the Scottish dressing-room from Irish partisans. It was a death threat . . . Gallacher would be shot if he did not ease up. Hughie of course ignored the threat and continued

Hughie Gallacher was quickly to become Scotland's regular centre-forward.

his scoring and exhibition play until the final whistle. The extremist home fans were not to be taken lightly though. Before the Scottish party sailed for the mainland, Hughie ventured to visit friends in the city. He was warned to be careful – Ireland was no place for strangers then, as now. He grinned, until a bullet splattered on a nearby wall as he walked near Queen's Bridge. Whether it was a real attempt on his life or a grim practical joke will never be known. Gallacher, always a humorous and witty character, could see the funny side afterwards. He remarked, "I'll have to extend my stay in Belfast. It seems I still haven't managed to teach the Irish how to shoot straight!" However, he was shocked at the incident. He recalled, "If ever a world record was set up for the 100 yards, I did it then. I never showed myself out until it was time to move homewards."

Remarkable stories surround Hughie Gallacher's life from his earliest days kicking a tanner ba' around the streets of Bellshill. He was born in the Lanark mining town in 1903, the son of a Protestant Irishman. It was a rugged community Gallacher was brought up in, like many in industrial Scotland. The town loved football and young Gallacher played continually, kicking almost anything that moved . . . stones, cans, even a bundle of rags tied together, such was the rarity of owning a real football in those days.

At school he played in most positions, winning a Cup medal as a goalkeeper, and one of his companions was none other than Alex James, from nearby Mossend, another youngster to become a huge personality in years to come. Gallacher said of the friendship, "We used to kick anything we could lay our hands on," while James noted, "Hugh and I hit it off right from the start. We scrapped together and dogged together and we romped the streets together."

The two tiny tots were brought up worshipping the grand Celtic XI of just before World War One. They adored Patsy Gallacher in particular and both players modelled much of their style on the Celtic ace. Gallacher worked down the coal-pit on leaving school and apart from playing football for local sides Tannochside Athletic and Hattonrigg Thistle, also took up boxing. He was friendly with Johnny Brown and Tommy Milligan, both to become professional champions. He sparred on a regular basis and was never afraid of the bigger man. Hughie Gallacher was strong, aggressive and short-tempered. He certainly had the right background for the pugnacious game he was to play in years ahead.

Bellshill Athletic approached Gallacher in March 1920 and the youngster jumped at the chance of joining one of Scotland's top junior outfits. Now operating at centre-forward, he quickly made an impression in that standard of football. He found the net every other match and boasted a growing reputation. However, before Gallacher made his next step in a footballing career, the first of many controversial incidents took place. At barely 17 years of age he was married, a brief and stormy relationship which broke the Protestant-Catholic divide, so strong in Bellshill then. Tragically, his son died before he was 12 months old and the ramifications of that marriage were to stay with Hughie for over a decade.

On the football field he found happier days. In December 1920 he appeared for Scotland's junior side and grabbed an equaliser against Ireland. Only a matter of days afterwards he became a Queen of the South player, on his way to reaching a full-time professional career in Scottish football. He obtained a £30 signing-on fee and £5 per week in wages from a club not yet in the Scottish League, but, importantly, they played several reserve sides of established clubs. He was one step from first-class soccer.

Gallacher netted four goals on his first appearance in a blue and white Queen's shirt and continued creating headline after headline in a short, but very productive, stay at Palmerston Park. He registered 19 goals in only nine games and had several scouts watching his developing talent. St Mirren's Johnny Cochrane wanted him and so did Airdrie, especially after Hughie had grabbed a wonderful goal against their second string.

Gallacher in his early days at Broomfield Park, Airdrie.

Queen of the South had little hope of keeping his services, but before Gallacher could make a move he was in the news again, rushed to hospital suffering from double pneumonia. Hughie was in a bad way, placed on the danger list for a few days at Dumfries Infirmary. He was laid up for five weeks and doctors even said they thought he would never play football again. Gallacher made the comment, "It seemed my brief tilt at fame was finished."

Fame, though, was just beginning for Hughie Gallacher. Once he recovered, Airdrieonians made a swift move for the titch of a man with a hunger for goals. Gallacher was 18 years old and in May 1921 joined what was then a mediocre Division One side. However in the coming years the Broomfield club gradually built a team to challenge the Glasgow Old Firm and Gallacher played a key role, grabbing a century of goals for the Waysiders.

After a two-year apprenticeship, Gallacher became a regular in Airdrie's side for season 1922/23. The Diamonds finished as runners-up to Rangers and a formidable team had taken shape. Jimmy Reid was a commanding veteran, Willie Russell a dainty schemer, while outside-left Jimmy Somerville was able to get goals as well as make them. Into the side came teenager Bob McPhail, to develop into a prodigious talent like Gallacher. Other members of Airdrie's fine side were Jock Ewart, a goalkeeper of international standard, centre-half Jackie McDougall, a Scotland player too, and Bob Bennie, another to be honoured by his country.

Gallacher and his colleagues made headlines as a new force in Scottish football. Gallacher was highly praised but was also often in trouble with referees and defenders who crashed into the little forward with regular brutality. Gallacher's whiplash tongue and ever-lit short temper often caused fiery moments on the field . . . and gave him even more publicity.

Hughie was a difficult individual, more so for the opposition but also at times for his team-mates. Bob McPhail noted in his biography, "He was a selfish wee fellow, he thought of no one but himself. He had a vicious tongue and he used it on opponents. I learned swear words from Hughie I had never heard before."

In season 1923/24 Airdrie again ended as second club to Rangers. Highlight of the season was a 6-1 victory over Clyde, in a game that saw Gallacher net five goals. His finish was deadly and as the *Daily Record* noted, "Defenders don't get much time for thinking when Hughie is about." It was the first of six occasions on which the centre-forward netted five goals in a single fixture.

In 1924 Airdrie also won the Scottish Cup for the first and up to now only time, after an extraordinary run to the final which saw tough battles with Morton, Ayr United – a tie which lasted almost seven hours – and Falkirk. In the final at Ibrox Park, Airdrie faced Hibernian and with a commanding performance, won the trophy through two headers from Russell. Bob McPhail recalled that "the terrier-like attitude of Gallacher caused havoc with the Hibs defence".

Gallacher had also been petitioned for a Scotland call-up. Airdrie's success had flung him into the news and his stature broadened the more he was seen. Scoring 39 goals that season, he earned his first cap against Northern Ireland, playing alongside his Broomfield team-mate Jimmy Reid. Hughie had just celebrated his 21st birthday and performed well

Newcastle paid a record fee of £6,500 to take the goalscoring ace to Tyneside in 1925.

in a 2-0 victory. The *Daily Record* wrote, "Hugh Gallacher of Airdrie made many friends – yes, Gallacher is worthy of another trial." Hughie was on his way to becoming Scotland's next centre-forward.

Gallacher was now a feared striker. He possessed remarkable ball control and had confidence second to none, almost to the point of being conceited and boastful. He had the talent to perform the unexpected and could swerve, feint and slip past players at ease. Gallacher was dangerous from any position, scoring from seemingly impossible angles. His shooting was perhaps his greatest natural gift. Hughie possessed amazing strength in his short, stocky legs and could poke a ball with immense power without much of a backswing. For his size Gallacher was also deceptively good in the air, outjumping much taller markers and frequently scoring with a subtle flick of the forehead.

Yet he was not only goaltaker-in-chief, but a provider too. He laid on countless chances by a deft pass or flash of dribbling skill. Apart from all the classic touches, Hughie possessed stamina and gritty determination, qualities not usually associated with skilled ball players. It was his variety of play that made him such a menace.

Success and fame brought problems though. The battering and heavy challenges from defenders continued and became commonplace as the non-skilled resorted to any tactic to stop his thrusts. It would get worse too when he moved to England. Hughie's legs became a constant mass of scars, bumps and a colour varying from blue to purple to black. Hughie, though, had to learn to live with the rough stuff. He started wearing a three-quarter-inch thick pad of cotton wool under his shin pads and took punishment with remarkable guts. He bewildered opponents by coming back again and again for more. But he could never stop retaliating or blaming referees for lack of protection. Hughie never mastered his temper and flare-ups were the norm when Gallacher was around.

The season after Airdrie's Cup success, 1924/25, Hughie again represented Scotland and made the centre-forward spot his own with a series of stunning exhibitions. Gallacher put on a magnificent show against Wales, scoring two goals – his second, a solo effort, was talked about for years. There were five defenders between the centre-forward and the goal. A lightning burst and he streaked upfield, the ball seemingly tied to his boot. He swerved past one man, then the next. Another Welshman raced up to him, but Hughie left him perplexed. Only Gray, Oldham Athletic's Welsh 'keeper stood between him and the goal of a lifetime. Gray came out and dived frantically for the ball. Hughie coolly hooked it over the goalkeeper's body and tapped it into the net. Gallacher rated that goal as his best ever and recalled, "As I turned to walk back I saw the Welsh players applauding me."

He was now Scotland's number one choice for the next few seasons, without a rival despite Jimmy McGrory's amazing scoring record in League football. Gallacher holds formidable statistics in a blue Scotland shirt, netting 24 goals in only 20 games. Only Kenny Dagleish and Dennis Law have scored more goals, and in many more outings. Included was another record five-goal strike in Belfast, this time in 1929, for the full national side. And all this after another sensational story hit the press, proclaiming he was not eligible to even play for the Scots, because he was not Scottish at all, but Irish by birth! A real fuss was caused until Hughie's original birth certificate, verifying his nationality, was rushed to Scotland's headquarters by his indignant mother.

Many an English club raided the Border to watch him. All of Airdrie's

At Stamford Bridge, Hughie teamed up with Alec Jackson. They are seen here together after a training stint.

star players eventually moved to bigger clubs and Gallacher was no exception, being the pick of the side. Newcastle United were the club that became very determined to acquire his talents. In December 1925 they paid what was reported as £6,500, although the fee was rumoured to be as high as £7,000, a new record. Tyneside's press heralded Gallacher's arrival as the coup of the decade: "Newcastle United Football Club has effected the smartest stroke of football business that has been transacted in modern times."

The 22-year-old joined a more than competent Newcastle squad. They had won the FA Cup in 1924 and had consistently finished high in Division One since the First World War. Gallacher immediately made an impact in England and started piling up the goals, netting over 300 in the coming years. Hughie scored two on his début, 15 in his first nine games, 34 in the season and, as newly appointed skipper of United, netted a record 36 goals in only 38 games as the club won the League Championship in 1926/27.

Gallacher was idolised on Tyneside like no other. Only Jackie Milburn, another Number 9 star, could equal his popularity in years to come. Hughie loved the Geordie hero worship. He marched proudly round the pubs and clubs of Tyneside snappily decked out in trendy suits and white spats, and often with a white fedora or black bowler. A complete Twenties dandy, he adored being recognised and loved signing autographs. The razzmatazz was made for him, although Gallacher never lost his working-class roots. He always had a feeling for the underprivileged, and frequently helped down-and-outs. There was a soft-hearted individual and kind character behind the glamorous facade.

Alongside Hughie at St James Park were plenty of fellow Scots. Tom McDonald and Bob McKay were both ex-Rangers men at inside-forward. Goalkeeper Willie Wilson hailed from Edinburgh, Willie Gibson and Roddy McKenzie, two powerful wing-halves, were from north of the Border too. Gibson was brother of Jimmy, Gallacher's colleague in the Wizards' team. Tommy Lang, Jimmy Boyd and Willie Chalmers all came from Gallacher country near Bellshill, as did Jimmy Low and Joe Harris. It was home from home. Other established pros at Gallowgate included Tommy Urwin and Stan Seymour, both England international wingers, while Frank Hudspeth and Charlie Spencer were two defenders who also turned out for the English.

For the next three seasons Gallacher was at the zenith of his career and his boundless talent showed wherever he played. Of course he made headlines for the wrong reasons too. But that was Hughie Gallacher. He ended up in court after a punch-up under the flickering gas lights of one of the Tyne's bridges and there were stories of excessive drinking habits, even to the point of having to be collected from a local pub to get changed for a United fixture. He was suspended by the Football Association for two months for a much publicised row with celebrated referee Bert Fogg . . . an irate Gallacher ending up kicking the official into the bath after a fiery 90 minutes with Huddersfield Town.

More clashes with referees followed. Hughie could never resist back-chatting to the man with the whistle and was handed a reputation by officials up and down the country, Hughie claiming they victimised him. He was in more trouble with the Football Association after writing

Gallacher, with his wife, leaves court after being discharged from bankruptcy in 1935.

a series of controversial articles, and on a summer tour was firstly sent off in Italy and given an armed escort, then accused of being drunk and disorderly on the pitch by annoyed Hungarians. Gallacher just could not keep out of the news.

Despite scoring plenty of goals for the Magpies, over 140 in only 174 games, his constant brushes with officialdom, including several with United's hierarchy, caused a serious rift between Hughie and some of Newcastle's board of directors. Transfer speculation began and a fierce debate raged in the north-east of England. Gallacher did not want to leave, the fans didn't want to lose him, but apparently the club and new manager, ex-Ranger Andy Cunningham, wanted to cash in. Chelsea made a massive bid of £10,000 in the summer months of 1930 and, without Hughie knowing a thing about it, a deal was concluded and Gallacher was dispatched to Stamford Bridge to his annoyance.

Hughie was reported as saying, "I did well at Airdrie, I have done well at Newcastle. I'll do well anywhere." And so he did. With Chelsea, although he never quite matched his game-by-game form or popularity as he had done at Broomfield or St James Park, Gallacher was still a formidable opponent, still an amazing character and still often in trouble.

Gallacher teamed up with Alec Jackson and Tommy Law at Chelsea, and with Alec Cheyne, Andy Wilson and a host of other Scots in London, including his school chum, Alex James, then at Arsenal. In only his second game he was responsible for remarkable crowd scenes back on Tyneside. His ever faithful Geordie fans flocked into Newcastle's ground to see their departed hero return with Chelsea. A record crowd of 68,386 was established, a figure unlikely to be beaten. A further 10,000 were locked out.

He was in trouble with officials again; as the object of some vicious handling, he retaliated and hurled scowls at several referees. On one such occasion Gallacher was sent off and suspended for another long period. Hughie later said, "Once again my hasty tongue had got me in trouble." But it was not all bad. He skippered Chelsea on an FA Cup run in 1931/32 which almost ended up back at Wembley for the stormy Scot. Chelsea won a semi-final place after toppling Tranmere Rovers, West Ham United, Sheffield Wednesday and Liverpool. In the hat for the draw with Chelsea were Manchester City, London neighbours Arsenal and Gallacher's former club Newcastle United. And yes, fate saw to it that Chelsea came out with the Tynesiders.

At Leeds Road, Huddersfield, Newcastle went 2-0 ahead within the first 25 minutes but Chelsea rallied, spurred on by Gallacher who always raised his game against the Magpies. Before half-time Gallacher picked up a bad back-pass. He darted forward and in a flash the ball was in the net. But despite periods of intense pressure the Cockneys could not get an equaliser. It was the closest Hughie came to winning anything when at Stamford Bridge, in fact more often than not he was the key to relegation survival for the Blues.

The nightlife of London's West End frequently saw Gallacher's presence. He often ventured out and became involved in unsavoury incidents. Once, in a café in Fulham, Hughie was caught up in an argument . . . about football, what else? . . . and events became ugly. Gallacher, with a black-eye, was eventually arrested for disorderly conduct and hoisted off to jail. He was branded a troublemaker, even a drunk, and his days in the capital became increasingly difficult. He was offered bribes and illegal bonus payments from hangers-on and was at the centre of a major row with his club over money, along with friend Alec Jackson. The controversial treatment and departure of his Wembley Wizard colleague created a rift between club and player. Gallacher was to leave Stamford Bridge at the earliest opportunity.

Captain of Notts County, Gallacher almost led his side to promotion.

Now past 30 years of age, there was much transfer talk and, after deals fell through with Everton and Sunderland, Gallacher signed for Derby County in November 1934 for £2,750. The transfer ended up in more headlines, as several years later, when Derby had to face a major Football Association investigation over transfer irregularities which saw their respected boss George Jobey suspended *sine die*; it was claimed Hughie received an illegal £300 signing-on gift.

Before Gallacher's departure from London, he went through disturbing court appearances, first, at last finalising a long running divorce, and then being declared a bankrupt. More happily, he remarried and saw his move to the Baseball Ground as a fresh start.

Throughout the Thirties, Derby County were one of England's finest sides and Gallacher stepped into a role vacated by the injured Jack Bowers, an international and another prolific goalscorer. Immediately the Scottish centre-forward, now thinning on top, created news. He netted on his début and was playing as well as at any period in his career. In the space of three weeks Hughie scored on nine occasions. Against Blackburn Rovers he claimed all of Derby's goals in a 5-2 victory.

The Rams challenged Arsenal and Sunderland for the title in both 1934/35 and 1935/36 seasons. They failed to lift the trophy on each occasion, finishing runners-up in 1936, with Gallacher in those two years collecting 40 goals in 55 games, a remarkable record for a man who was now classed as a veteran.

With Bowers returned to full fitness, Gallacher had completed his job and was off to a new club again in September 1936, this time a short distance to join Notts County where he soon teamed up with his old Scotland captain Jimmy McMullan, who was shortly to become manager at Meadow Lane. The Gallacher and McMullan partnership worked well for the Trent club, who were aiming to rid themselves of the Third Division stigma. Gallacher grabbed goals as if he was only 23 and not ten years senior and County shot up the table. They became favourites for promotion and gates increased dramatically as crowds packed in to see Gallacher in goals' mood. But just as had occurred at the Baseball Ground, Hughie failed, County ending in second place to Luton Town who clinched the only promotion spot. However, his season was a personal triumph. Gallacher filled the back pages again, scoring another 32 goals in just 46 games.

Becoming something of a suitcase footballer, Hughie was off on his travels as soon as McMullan left the club in December 1937. Again several clubs were interested in his talents and vast experience, despite his difficult reputation. A month later, as the new year opened, Gallacher moved back into the First Division with Grimsby Town, managed by Charlie Spencer, one of Hughie's team-mates at Newcastle. The Mariners were in the middle of a relegation struggle and Hughie was to be an emergency gamble as a replacement for another injured centre-forward, Pat Glover, again a noted international. The ploy worked a treat at Derby, but at Blundell Park Hughie never really fitted in, although Grimsby regained their First Division place by the end of the season. In fact, Gallacher clashed with Spencer and also ended up in the dock of the local court, banned from driving for a year and fined £12 after being found guilty of driving with alcohol in his bloodstream. Another transfer quickly followed.

Hughie Gallacher's final bow in the game was back on Tyneside,

The veteran Gallacher, 38 years old, with Gateshead just before the Second World War in 1939.

the region that adopted him and which he loved so much. In June 1938, for a mere £500, he joined Gateshead, then a club striving to reach Second Division status from Division Three. Public interest at Gallacher's nostalgic return was immense in the north-east. The man's charisma was phenomenal and Gateshead, for once, even overshadowed giants Newcastle United and Sunderland.

At the twilight of his career – Gallacher was almost 36 – he still possessed finesse on the ball and that ability born to him, the knack of scoring goals. With Gateshead he bagged 18 in the season, including another amazing five-goal strike in a match against Rotherham who felt the force of Hughie's size-six boots.

Gallacher finally called it a day after three games of the following season. It was not of his own accord, but because of war. He played his last game on 2 September 1939 at unglamorous Sincell Bank, home of Lincoln City. No doubt, but for Hitler and his Panzer forces, Hughie would have played on until he dropped. He was devoted to the game – but now that was all over.

Hughie Gallacher was both adored and loathed by differing factions of players and spectators. Every conceivable accolade and rebuke was heaped upon him. He was master opportunist and rip-roaring genius rolled into one. Gallacher, though, was not just to disappear from the limelight like so many stars. After serving as an ambulance driver during the war, he settled in Gateshead working in local factories – this after an unsuccessful bid to get a job in football, with clubs shunning his undoubted experience and knowledge, due to fear of controversial outbursts.

He was now a working-class Geordie. Gone were the flashy suits and bowler hat. Hughie now wore overalls and the traditional cloth-cap. Gallacher did a spot of newspaper work, reporting on north-east football, and he still managed to create news himself by being critical of his old club, Newcastle United. The Magpies responded by withdrawing ground-passes from the Scot. He also coached local sides, refereed games and got himself into bother with the Football Association once more after taking charge of a non-affiliated charity game at Berwick.

Gallacher's life was one with few mundane moments. Drama and incident followed him around and he created probably the biggest headline of all in 1957 through his own sad and dreadful demise.

Having lost his wife through illness, Hughie deteriorated rapidly. He drank heavily and found few real friends, only those who wished to fill him with alcohol. In May of 1957 he was charged with assault and ill treatment of his youngest son, and on Wednesday 12 June, Gallacher was summoned to appear before Gateshead Magistrates Court. But for Hughie, 12 June never came. His glittering career was far from his mind, he thought only of an unfortunate life and the prospect of facing a court on the most degrading of charges with public and press in full view. It was an ordeal he could not face.

Gallacher, perhaps Scotland's greatest ever centre-forward, jumped in front of the York-Edinburgh express train as it sped past on a line near his home. His decapitated body was found at the ironically named Dead Man's Crossing in Gateshead. He was 54 years old. The news of the manner of Gallacher's death was a shock to all in the game.

His had been an inspiring, sometimes notorious life and tragic in its ending. Hughie Gallacher is one Wembley Wizard who will be remembered as long as football is played. He was a one-off. His unpredictable and explosive temperament merely added to the fascination of the man and made him an even bigger box-office attraction. Hughie Gallacher had made news to the end. One newspaper headline read, "Hughie of the Magic Feet is Dead". There will never be another like him.

HUGH KILPATRICK GALLACHER

Career Span: 1920 to 1939
Born: Bellshill, Lanarkshire, 2 February 1903
Died: Gateshead, 11 June 1957
Career: Hattonrigg Thistle; Tannochside Athletic; Bellshill Athletic, 1920; Queen of the South, 1920; Airdrieonians, 1921; Newcastle United, 1925; Chelsea, 1930; Derby County, 1934; Notts County, 1936; Grimsby Town, 1938; Gateshead, 1938; Retired 1939
Club Honours:
Football League Champions, 1927
Football League Runners-up, 1936
Scottish League Runners-up, 1923, 1924, 1925
Scottish Cup winner, 1924
Full Internationals: 20 appearances, 24 goals, 1924-1935
1923/24 v N Ireland
1924/25 v Wales(2), N Ireland (1), England (2)
1925/26 v Wales, N Ireland (3), England
1926/27 v Wales (1), N Ireland, England
1927/28 v Wales (1), England
1928/29 v Wales (3), N Ireland (5), England
1929/30 v Wales (2), N Ireland (2), France (2)
1933/34 v England
1934/35 v England
Scottish League XI: Two appearances, six goals 1925
1924/25 v Football League (1)
1925/26 v Irish League (5)
Unofficial Internationals: Six appearances, ten goals
Scottish tour of N. America, 1935
Junior International: One appearance, one goal, 1920

MATCH ANALYSIS

Season	Club	League app-gls	Cup app-gls	Scotland app-gls	Other represent- ative app-gls	Total app-gls
1920-21 Queen of the South		—	1-1	—	—	1-1
1921-22 Airdrie (Div 1)		11-7	4-0	—	—	15-7
1922-23 Airdrie (Div 1)		18-9	2-1	—	—	20-10
1923-24 Airdrie (Div 1)		34-33	9-6	1-0	—	44-39
1924-25 Airdrie (Div 1)		32-32	3-3	3-5	2-6	40-46
1925-26 Airdrie (Div 1)		16-9	—	1-0	1-5	18-14
1925-26 Newcastle Utd (Div 1)		19-23	3-2	2-3	—	24-28
1926-27 Newcastle Utd (Div 1)		38-36	3-3	3-1	—	44-40
1927-28 Newcastle Utd (Div 1)		32-21	1-0	2-1	—	35-22
1928-29 Newcastle Utd (Div 1)		33-24	1-0	3-8	—	37-32
1929-30 Newcastle Utd (Div 1)		38-29	6-5	3-6	—	47-40
1930-31 Chelsea (Div 1)		30-14	1-0	—	—	31-14
1931-32 Chelsea (Div 1)		36-24	5-6	—	—	41-30
1932-33 Chelsea (Div 1)		36-19	1-0	—	—	37-19
1933-34 Chelsea (Div 1)		23-13	5-3	1-0	—	29-16
1934-35 Chelsea (Div 1)		7-2	—	—	—	7-2
1934-35 Derby County (Div 1)		27-23	3-1	1-0	6-10	37-34
1935-36 Derby County (Div 1)		24-15	1-1	—	—	25-16
1936-37 Notts County (Div 3)		32-25	1-0	—	—	33-25
1937-38 Notts County (Div 3)		13-7	—	—	—	13-7
1937-38 Grimsby Town (Div 1)		12-3	—	—	—	12-3
1938-39 Gateshead (Div 3)		31-18	—	—	—	31-18
1939-40 Gateshead (Div 3)		3-0	—	—	—	3-0
Total		545-386	50-32	20-24	9-21	624-463

12

ALEX JAMES . . . AND THOSE BAGGY SHORTS

He diddled, danced, dodged and put his opponents in a maze.
The Bulletin, March 1928

BELLSHILL IN Lanarkshire boasts little to put the town into the spotlight. It is a hardworking and honest community not far from Glasgow. Yet it should raise a statue to its Wembley Wizard heroes, the district's most famous sons. Not only did Hughie Gallacher hail from Bellshill, but his colleague in Scotland's forward line, Alex James, was also born there, in Mossend, one of four villages to make up the town. Few places, if any, the size of Bellshill boast such footballing talent . . . two of the biggest names ever to appear for Scotland.

Alex James was as idolised and well-known as his school chum Gallacher during the era between the wars. There were no bigger personalities north or south of the border. James was a late developer but reached fame as the master architect behind Arsenal's formidable success in the Thirties. He was renowned throughout the country as the genius at inside-forward in long baggy shorts, a comic Chaplinesque-looking figure of football. His flapping, oversized white shorts have characterized James to this day. They were his trademark.

James was another little 'un, only five feet six inches in height and, just like Gallacher, he was an unpredictable and volatile Scots personality. They were in many ways two of the same breed. They had the same rugged background, were rebellious and questioned authority frequently. They were extroverts, somewhat conceited and had a perky humour. Yet they were natural footballers.

James, the more refined and well-spoken of the pair, was born the son of a railway worker just after the turn of the century. He was one of five children and attended Bellshill Academy along with Gallacher. The two stars of the future were far from classroom swots, rather more inclined to be in the playground with a ball at their feet. They frequently played truant and by the time James was in his teens he avoided learning a trade, working instead in a munitions factory where he received a nasty facial scar and the sack after a work prank. Then Alex became an office clerk. By that time he had dedicated himself to football although, unlike his friend Gallacher, who rose to fame quite rapidly, the youngster found progress slow.

Alex James left school in 1916 and played with local sides Brandon Amateurs and Orbiston Celtic, a tough outfit known as the 'Cannibals'.

Alex James. Many reckoned he was the best inside-forward there has ever been.

One of the kids that watched Orbiston in those days was a schoolboy called Matt Busby who looked after the players' kit, James's included. Alex entered a better grade of football when he was asked to sign for junior club Glasgow Ashfield in 1921. He received all of five shillings a week and no bonus. James, though, was delighted. Ashfield were one of the aristocrats of the non-League game, having just won three major junior trophies. Jimmy Gibson, to star with James at Wembley, had just graduated from Ashfield to Partick Thistle.

Alex settled at inside-right and despite his new club's poor form – Ashfield slipped dramatically from the top – his displays of, at times, brilliant footwork with the ball, prompted several League managers to have a look at him. Motherwell offered James a trial and the small youth turned out for the reserve team but was dwarfed by both his colleagues and the opposition. He was completely overawed and it was back to Saracen Park and Glasgow Ashfield for the youngster who still possessed a very much schoolboyish appearance.

It wasn't long though before other clubs offered him a second chance. He travelled to Tynecastle but Hearts turned him down for being too small, then Raith Rovers director Robert Morrison spotted him playing for a Glasgow junior select side. Morrison was to be the man to give James another opportunity, and to help him through some

Raith Rovers in 1924. Back row, left to right: *Morris, Marchbank, Barton, McKenzie, Innes, Chapman.* Front row: *Bell, Neish, Miller, James, Ritchie.*

early troubled days. In June 1922, at 21 years old, he signed for the Fife club.

Although never a football hotbed, the town of Kirkcaldy had just seen Raith challenge Rangers and Celtic for the League Championship in season 1921/22. They finished third, the club's highest ever placing and James was soon in senior action due to a crop of injuries. He made his Scottish League début against Celtic at Parkhead in September 1922, up against his boyhood idol Patsy Gallacher. He quickly faced Airdrie then and the other Gallacher, Hughie. However, Alex found first-team football tough. John Harding, in his biography of the star noted, "James quickly proved to be something of a prima donna: a mixture of arrogance, wounded pride and no little cheek." He also had problems with his physique. Not only was James small, but he was also slightly-built, easily knocked off the ball. Raith's trainer, Dave Willis, an ex-Newcastle and Sunderland player, spent many hours building him up. He even placed the budding footballer on a diet of cod-liver oil. It was sickening stuff, James was to say, but over a period it helped to thicken him out and was of great benefit in the future.

Willis also helped the youngster get through a severe problem of feeling the cold. James hated the winter months and freezing conditions. He was affected by rheumatism most of his adult life and was rubbed down with a liniment of camphor, peanut oil and whisky before a game, to reduce the affects of chill air! He even wore white long-johns under his strip and looked anything but a superstar to be. This weakness was also one of the reasons he wore long shorts. James said, "The pants kept my knees warm on a cold day."

Over the first few months James found that difficulties mounted at Starks Park. Many of the club's directors had doubts about both his physique and attitude, but Robert Morrison had none. He saw hidden genius in Alex, and was determined to persevere with his find. Gradually Morrison's judgement was proved good – extremely good – as James slowly developed into an inside-forward of exceptional ability.

Raith Rovers finished ninth in Alex's first season in League football, and fourth in his second, season 1923/24. Rovers had by then put together a forward line to be the talk of the country, albeit for only a short time. They were known as Raith's 'Famous Five', all imports to Starks Park. Englishman Peter Bell was at outside-right, George Miller, ex-Hearts and Scotland, at inside-right and the tall Tom Jennings at centre-forward, a high calibre leader later to join Leeds United. James had now settled at inside-left and he teamed up with Bobby Archibald, a bow-legged winger from Aberdeen. They knitted together perfectly and at one stage in 1925, Millwall, then in England's Third Division, offered to buy the whole line *en bloc* for a massive sum of £50,000 . . . or so it was rumoured. This was before the first transfer fee of £10,000 had been established. The deal never materialised but the "£50,000 forward-line" tag stuck.

Dave Morris, Scotland's captain in that year, was also in the Raith line-up, as was Bill Collier, and also John Duncan, who had just left to join Leicester City for a large fee. They had both appeared for Scotland too. The Rovers squad went on a foreign close-season tour and James found himself shipwrecked off the coast of Spain *en route* for the Canary Islands. Their steamer, the *Highland Loch*, bound for South America was grounded by the captain in bad weather and marooned beside a small fishing village. It was quite an experience for the lad from the pits of Lanarkshire; rarely had James travelled far and here was his first voyage abroad almost ending in catastrophe. This was perhaps the reason he was to dislike journeys immensely, always in future years being a bad traveller to games far afield, especially by sea.

James had now established himself as one of Scotland's up-and-coming stars, even a possible challenger to Tommy Cairns in the national side and he was selected for an international trial. With Raith he was a sharp-shooting inside-left, able to find the net with spectacular long-range efforts that had venom and accuracy. He also frequently set off on elaborate dribbles with the ball, spasms of sheer brilliant individuality. One pen picture of the day noted "a deceptive swerve, wonderful footcraft, and great power of ball control give James a most captivating style". He was also an incessant talker on the field, a chatterbox. Jimmy McMullan once said, "Alex James's tongue went like a gramophone from the kick-off." Alex loved a verbal fight and was often in trouble with referees during his early years and, like Hughie Gallacher, he was, alas, the victim of many fouls by opposing defenders.

He was sent off in two successive matches during the 1923/24 season, both after clashes with rivals and protests to the official in charge. However his overriding abilities as a linkman and potential matchwinner attracted many club representatives to Rovers' games. One such scout was Jimmy Lawrence, the former Scotland goalkeeper, then with Preston North End. He was impressed with the emerging schemer and sent a glowing report to Deepdale.

Alex opened the new 1925/26 season a Raith player but after only four games of the campaign were completed he was meeting Preston officials at the Station Hotel in Kirkcaldy. James signed for the English Second Division club in September 1925 for a £3,250 fee, becoming one of the virtual exodus of Scottish talent to cross the Border at that time. Included were Jackson, Gallacher and, soon after, Jimmy McMullan.

North End had attempted to obtain James's signature twice during the summer break but had been thwarted by Raith directors. Leading their negotiations was James Taylor, a figurehead at Preston who had been captivated by the James style. He said to the player after watching him as the season opened, "I was tremendously impressed and made up my mind that I must definitely have you at all costs." Taylor was persistent and acquired his man, who was to become an important piece in his master plan to regain First Division status. Preston had a distinct fancy for Scots then, as they always had since the days of their inroads into Scotland's amateur game before the turn of the century. More money was spent – over £12,000 on imports from north of Carlisle. James had plenty of fellow countrymen as first-team regulars. Included were his former Raith centre-half, Dave Morris, signed for £4,700, ex-Airdrie men, goalkeeper Jock Ewart and Willie Russell, while at outside-right was Bathgate-born Alec Reid. Walter Jackson, brother of Alec, arrived from Aberdeen and Tom Gillespie came from Hearts.

However, despite considerable talent which also included England centre-forward Tom Roberts, Preston never achieved anything in either League or Cup competitions. The 1927/28 season was the closest James and his Preston side came to reaching the First Division. They made a strong promotion bid, scoring a century of goals, in which Alex was both goalmaker and goaltaker, netting 18 that year. They were an attractive side and gates soared at Deepdale and at grounds around the Second

A move to Preston North End came for James in 1925. There he joined forces with his former Raith captain, Dave Morris, and ex-Airdrie star Willie Russell.

Division. James became a personality player and Preston were often referred to as "Alex James and ten others". They were something of a one-man team in many fans' eyes.

Preston, though, failed to win promotion, finishing in fourth place, but at least James had pushed himself into the Scotland reckoning with consistent displays. He had been capped for the first time back in October 1925 at Ninian Park, Cardiff, where he partnered Hughie Gallacher against the Welsh. That was the first of only eight appearances for his country, a remarkably small number of caps for a player rated by many as the best inside-forward there has been. George Stevenson, Motherwell's great servant, and Bob McPhail of Rangers were his main rivals for the Scotland shirt and the Ibrox man was selected more often than not, to James's annoyance.

The peak of his Scotland career was at Wembley in 1928 and immediately after when he dislodged McPhail from the inside-left berth. James's marvellous two-goal strike in the Wizards' match prompted another transfer move to take place in the not too distant future. His name had gone down in the notebook of an eminent manager. On the international front, though, his quick thinking and slick passing were lost to the stage because of cross-Border selection problems just at a time when he was playing his best football. An additional problem for

James moved to the First Division stage in 1930 and began his long association with Arsenal.

James's Scotland prospects was that he once shunned the selectors and turned his back on his country when he dropped out of a clash with England because of injury but controversially managed to play for his club on the same day.

With Preston seemingly unable to get out of Division Two it was only a matter of time before a big transfer deal took James on to a level where his ability could be fully utilised. In June 1929 he moved to Arsenal after a row with Preston's directors over permission to play for Scotland, and a protracted transfer saga. James, now 27 years old, could not have found a bigger platform to display his sometimes staggering talent, for Highbury to be the focal point in English football for the next decade, although up to 1930 the Londoners had achieved little in the game to speak of. That was to change rapidly.

There was quite a scramble for the chubby-looking Scot who was now

Arsenal dominated the Thirties and James was the architect of their success. James is pictured here being chaired at Wembley after winning the FA Cup in 1936.

an ostentatious personality, immaculately dressed in flashy suits and hair in the style of a film star. His transfer caused major controversy and ultimately a Football League enquiry. Aston Villa were strong contenders, as were Liverpool and Manchester City, but Herbert Chapman, manager of the Gunners, saw James as the ideal linkman to partner English stalwart David Jack in midfield and pulled out all his tricks to take him to Highbury.

Football League officials were convinced that there must have been some extra inducement for James to sign for Arsenal. They were indeed correct in their assertion, but could do little about it. Chapman had arranged an additional job for his new midfield schemer, an appointment in Selfridge's department store on Oxford Street as a sports demonstrator at £250 per year. James also earned more money from writing for the *London Evening Star* and later the *Sunday Graphic*. His meagre footballing

Three Gunners – with James showing off those famous baggy shorts, flanked by David Jack (left) and Joe Hulme (right).

wage of £8 per week was considerably boosted. James cost Arsenal £8,750, another big signing by Chapman who had only a few months earlier broken the transfer record by bringing David Jack to London. The duo, though, repaid their massive fees over and over again as Arsenal began to monopolise English football.

The new season started with Alex facing Leeds United and his old Raith team-mate, Tom Jennings, at Highbury. Arsenal won 4-0 and the Cockneys went off like a rocket, recording five wins in their first six games. But a slump followed as the new Arsenal tactical game hit problems and Alex found life in Division One almost too much for him. He was hampered by an ankle injury and Chapman had changed his role. At first he didn't like the manager's new tactics at all. Up to joining Arsenal, James had always been something of a free-roving forward, playing most of his football around the opposition's penalty box and scoring frequently. At Starks Park he grabbed 28 goals, at Deepdale over 50. Chapman, though, didn't need that type of player. As ex-Arsenal

James, who played only a handful of games for Scotland.

favourite Charlie Buchan wrote, "Arsenal wanted a midfield schemer, not a goalscorer, however brilliant he might be."

Chapman insisted that James play an anchor role in no-man's-land in the middle of the field, usually in a deep position, picking up balls from defence and releasing accurate passes up front. David Jack was allowed more freedom to attack, James was not. He also instructed Alex to play a defensive game as and when it was needed, a concept totally foreign to the Scot's football philosophy. Alex once made the comment, "I am never going to chase an opponent in possession of the ball." Yet now he had to and his form dipped. He was often being caught in possession and he was heavily criticised by the Highbury crowd. Chapman dropped his big signing and it looked as though he could have a stormy time at Highbury.

However, to James's credit, the little man battled with the problems of being in and out of the side and he eventually fitted into the Highbury set-up. By the time the FA Cup fourth-round tie with Birmingham City

Alex often played in charity games after retirement. He is pictured here with his great chum Hughie Gallacher, for a match in South Shields. Both players were almost 50. Gallacher is in the centre of the front row and James to his left.

took place at the end of January, Alex had sorted out his role and started to provide Arsenal's forwards with a midfield supply line. Gone were the days of scoring goals – he only managed a handful each year for the Londoners in eight seasons. James was now a provider first and foremost, and in a deep position. He admitted that Chapman was right: "I had my rows with him but there was no greater manager in football," he said.

Arsenal disposed of Birmingham and went all the way to the final where they met Chapman's previous side, Huddersfield Town, the country's leading club. Alec Jackson, with fond memories of Wembley, was in the Yorkshire side's line-up, but it was to be Alex James who became the star of the 1930 Cup final, and the hero of Gunners' fans who had less than six months ago baited him. On the day a German Zeppelin flew high over the stadium and obscured the sun, Arsenal won the FA Cup for the first time, thanks largely to the bewildering skill James possessed with the ball. The *Daily Herald* noted, "James was here, there and everywhere. He was magnificent throughout."

After 17 minutes Arsenal were awarded a free-kick for a foul on the schemer 40 yards out. James took it himself, quickly, a ploy he used in Scotland but rarely was allowed to succeed with in England. But on this occasion the referee allowed play to flow. A swift pass to Bastin, a rapid return and James went past a defender. Before anyone could move the ball crashed into the Huddersfield goal. It was a tactic planned by Alex in the team bus on the way from Harrow to Wembley Stadium.

He was involved in Arsenal's second goal too. Seeing Lambert streaking through the middle, James struck an inch-perfect long pass and the dashing centre-forward did the rest. FA Cup victory – the start of ten years of supremacy for the Gunners. James didn't forget who had stood by him in the past for he sent his Cup winners' medal to Robert Morrison back in Kirkcaldy. A note read: "If there had been no Bob Morrison there would have been no Alex James."

Alex went on to appear for Arsenal on over 250 occasions and rarely played a bad game once his initial weeks were behind him. There were other noted inside-forwards of the Thirties, men like Raich Carter, Peter Doherty and team-mate David Jack, a tall and graceful schemer. But James shone above them all. With a nonchalance that was almost cheek, a wiggle of the hips and shuffle of his feet over the ball as if to backheel it, the little magician flashed past to leave defenders rooted to the spot. He was a showman and opponents never knew what to expect. Hughie Gallacher once commented, "Alex always had little tricks – and how effective they were."

He rarely got into shooting range in Arsenal colours, but his passing with either foot was incomparable. From deep positions he sprayed long balls all over the field. One colleague said, "Wee Alex was the master at turning defence into attack." James wasn't lithe or built like an athlete, as, say, Jackson was; he was compact, rounded and stocky. Jack Harkness described him as, "A small dumpy sort of character with short legs on a long body . . . surely nobody ever looked less like a footballer." Anyone could beat him over a long sprint, but he was nippy over the first, and crucial, ten yards as he challenged rivals.

Anticipating moves, sometimes thinking even three or four passes ahead, Alex was Chapman's mastermind on the pitch and it is certain that the club would not have achieved so much but for his skills. He was the very heart of Arsenal's side. The Londoner's success came from a policy of defence in depth with fast breakaways inspired by James's precision passing. They played the game differently from others with their wingers scoring goals rather than making them.

Arsenal's defence was marshalled by Herbie Roberts, red-haired and a towering stopper, while the smash-and-grab raids were made by the lightning trio of Hulme, Bastin and Lambert. Joe Hulme was one of the fastest wingers in the game and he thrilled crowds. Cliff Bastin, known as 'Boy' Bastin, burst on to the scene as an 18-year-old with ice-cool character. The two wingers scored over 200 goals for Arsenal in the following years. Jack Lambert was robust and an effective leader, the only one of a whole array of Arsenal stars not to be capped.

Other names to wear the red shirt of the Gunners alongside James were full-backs Tom Parker, George Male and the immaculate Eddie Hapgood, later England's captain. Jack Crayston and Wilf Copping were powerful wing-halves. Ray Bowden eventually replaced David Jack, while the big-hearted Ted Drake entered the scene along with Bob John, Charlie Jones and Dan Lewis, three Welshmen. Frank Moss, at Preston for a while with James, became Arsenal's 'keeper and Ireland's Jimmy Dunne and England's Bernard Joy took part in the success too. All were internationals.

The year after winning the FA Cup, Arsenal won the League Championship by a record margin of seven points. Again it was the first time Highbury had seen the trophy – in fact, surprisingly perhaps, the first occasion any London club had. They lost only four games, with James supplying a constant stream of telling passes that were converted in style by Lambert (38 goals), Jack (31), Bastin (28), and Hulme (14), the goalpoachers.

In season 1931/32 Arsenal were runners-up in both League and Cup competitions, James missing the Cup final and another Wembley appearance against Newcastle United because of a twisted knee. He had to sit disconsolately on the bench. In 1933 Alex was appointed Arsenal captain and suffered with the others the infamous giant-killing feat of Walsall, Arsenal's blackest day, before leading his team to another title victory. Arsenal settled the issue after a 3-1 victory over local rivals Chelsea in front of 74,190 fans at Stamford Bridge. Hughie Gallacher, in Chelsea's side, was one of the first to congratulate his friend on the Championship success.

The volatile side to Alex James's character then showed itself when he refused to play in an exhibition friendly with Cliftonville, and heated words were spoken between club and player. At a celebration gathering the Championship trophy was presented to another player, and not to skipper James who had failed to turn up. He wasn't the easiest of players to handle and apart from those two incidents had several tiffs with manager Chapman, refusing terms on more than one occasion. Money, or the lack of it in football, was as important to James as it was to the other Wembley Wizards. He held out for the best deal, legal or illegal, that he could extract from Arsenal. If Alex hadn't been such a key player to the Gunners, Chapman would never have stood for his antics. As it was James was allowed to disappear from training, miss friendly games, even to lie in bed until noon on occasions while his team-mates were breaking sweat on the training ground. He was given special treatment other players never received.

The row over the title presentation blew over, although Hapgood was handed the captaincy, and the League Championship remained in the Gunners' boardroom at the end of the following season, a year which brought James problems with injury and the great loss of Herbert Chapman who died after a short illness. It was a hat-trick of titles for Arsenal in 1935 and the first hat-trick of goals by James in a match against Sheffield Wednesday. He grabbed three in a stirring 20-minute spell, all apparently to show his nine-year-old son that he could in fact score, so rare were his goals then.

It was back to Wembley in 1936 to face Second Division promotion candidates Sheffield United. The media predicted Arsenal would win decisively but, as often happens in football, the underdogs raised their game. The Gunners won all right, through a James-inspired and Drake-finished goal, but one headline noted, "Arsenal scramble through". James, reinstated as skipper, climbed the steps and proudly lifted the Cup.

Arsenal continued to be a force in England until the outbreak of war. As the club's official centenary history observed, "By the time Hitler's war began, Arsenal were without doubt the greatest, the most famous, the most widely supported football club in the world." James was now well into his thirties and was slower. The opposition were now beginning to get the better of him. The 1936/37 season was to be his last.

James played his final game at Highbury against Bolton Wanderers on 1 May 1937, although he took part in a summer tour before quitting. His stay in north London was most rewarding. He won four Championship medals and took part in three Cup finals in the space of only eight seasons.

Alex didn't leave the Arsenal set-up altogether though and was often seen within the palatial marble walls of Highbury. James remained in London, in the bright lights he loved, still a star of the sporting world. He went into several business ventures that made little money, including such diverse activities as pig-farming and women's outfitting. He owned a sweet and tobacconist's shop near the Arsenal ground and became a director of a football pools company, which took him into direct conflict with the game's authorities. Betting on football had been outlawed by the Football Association and Football League, and when James became involved in attempting to introduce a pools system they clamped down on the former international, banning him from any involvement in the professional game. Alas, his company, Ring Pools, a rival to Littlewoods and Copes, folded quickly and he was left to concentrate on journalism, working as a personality football correspondent for the *News of the World* and also as an occasional broadcaster for the BBC. He was well liked and always had a cheery grin for all to see.

James, as was expected of a man who never allowed officials to walk over him, was controversial in some of his views. His memoirs were headed, "Football with the lid off! The truth of the Racket must be told", while another headline read, "Slave Markets of Soccer". They revealed the inside dealings of the football world, stories the game's hierarchy certainly did not want in the press. He was branded a troublemaker by many within the game.

Just before the outbreak of World War Two, Alex accepted a contract from the Polish Football Association to coach top players in Warsaw. He returned home a matter of days before Germany invaded the country, narrowly missing certain internment by Nazi forces. He served as a Gunner – fittingly, after playing for Arsenal – in the Maritime Royal Artillery Regiment during the fighting and attempted to play football again for Northampton in wartime leagues, but the FA held their ban and objected.

However, with peace restored the men at Lancaster Gate lifted their edict and Alex returned to Highbury as Arsenal's third-team coach, though he still retained his reporter's notepad. He was especially loud in praise of the modern game of football and pulled on a strip occasionally to play in charity games and testimonials, in more than one instance appearing alongside Hughie Gallacher in a Veterans' XI.

Like his Bellshill school friend, James was to die at a relatively young age. When he was 51 Alex was taken ill. Doctors thought he had contracted tuberculosis, but it turned out to be much worse. James had cancer. Through his old club's contacts, the King's Surgeon, Sir Bryce Thomas, attempted to save his life, but on 1 June 1953 he died in the Royal Northern Hospital, a short walk from Highbury.

Many said Alex James, with those ever famous baggy shorts, was the most celebrated schemer to play the game. George Allison, a later Arsenal manager remarked, "Alex was the greatest exponent of all the arts and crafts known to Association football." As a mark of his standing in the game his death warranted an obituary in *The Times*, a rarity in football. They observed that James had, "a smiling, chubby face which added to the picture of a player who looked quite unconcerned about the fortunes of a match". Alex James may have appeared far from looking like the ideal, athletic picture of a footballer, but he possessed abundant craft, Scottish craft at its very best.

ALEXANDER WILSON JAMES

Career Span: 1922 to 1937
Born: Mossend, Lanarkshire, 14 September 1901
Died: London, 1 June 1953
Career: Orbiston Celtic; Glasgow Ashfield, 1921; Raith Rovers, 1922; Preston North End, 1925; Arsenal, 1929; Retired, 1937
Club Honours:
Football League Champions 1931, 1933, 1934, 1935; Football League runners-up 1932
FA Cup winners 1930, 1936
Full Internationals: Eight appearances, three goals, 1925-33
1925/26 v Wales
1927/28 v England (2)
1928/29 v N Ireland, England
1929/30 v Wales (1), N Ireland, England
1932/33 v Wales

MATCH ANALYSIS

Season	Club	League app-gls	Cup app-gls	Scotland app-gls	Other represent- ative app-gls	Total app-gls
1922-23	Raith Rovers (Div 1)	25-5	4-1	—	—	29-6
1923-24	Raith Rovers (Div 1)	33-11	4-0	—	—	37-11
1924-25	Raith Rovers (Div 1)	36-11	4-0	—	—	40-11
1925-26	Raith Rovers (Div 1)	4-0	—	—	—	4-0
1925-26	Preston N.E. (Div 2)	34-14	2-0	1-0	—	37-14
1926-27	Preston N.E. (Div 2)	39-11	2-0	—	—	41-11
1927-28	Preston N.E. (Div 2)	38-18	1-0	1-2	—	40-20
1928-29	Preston N.E. (Div 2)	36-10	1-0	2-0	—	39-10
1929-30	Arsenal (Div 1)	31-6	6-1	3-1	—	40-8
1930-31	Arsenal (Div 1)	40-5	3-0	—	—	43-5
1931-32	Arsenal (Div 1)	32-2	5-0	—	—	37-2
1932-33	Arsenal (Div 1)	40-3	1-0	1-0	—	42-3
1933-34	Arsenal (Div 1)	22-3	0-0	—	—	22-3
1934-35	Arsenal (Div 1)	30-4	3-0	—	—	33-4
1935-36	Arsenal (Div 1)	17-2	6-0	—	—	23-2
1936-37	Arsenal (Div 1)	19-1	4-0	—	—	23-1
Total		476-106	46-2	8-3	—	530-111

13

ALAN MORTON . . . THE ORIGINAL 'WEE BLUE DEVIL'

I cannot recall an England back who mastered this little quiet modest man.
Sir Frederick Wall, Secretary of the FA, *50 Years of Football*

BOTH RANGERS Football Club and the Scottish national side have fielded many illustrious players, names that have gone down in football's annals as some of the greats. Few though were as respected both within the game and on the terraces as Alan Morton. He was idolised by the fans and held in reverence by fellow professionals, a player who hardly had a blemish on his name during a long career. Many reckoned he was the finest winger produced in the home countries, better even than Stanley Matthews. He was certainly the best at Ibrox Park, and undoubtedly in a Scotland shirt too.

No full-back could deaden his perplexing style. A naturally right-footed player, Morton operated at outside-left, and had the ability to use either foot. Slightly built, at nine-and-a-half stone at most, at less than five feet five inches another of the midget Wizards and he possessed an unusually long stride for such a small man and was deceptively fast. Morton had perfected a teasing cross, tantamount to a match-winner, that suddenly appeared to hang in the air and drop into the danger area. Charlie Buchan said of Morton: "Though on the small side, he had a wonderful way of slipping past the opposition." The former England star continued, "Morton's ball control, swerve and pinpoint accuracy in centring the ball have rarely been equalled."

The winger had defenders terrified at facing him, none more so than a whole line of England full-backs. They tried everything to stop him but Alan always had a particular relish when facing England's men. Ashurst, Goodhall and Cooper couldn't shackle him, neither could Clay, Longworth or Smart. The unfortunate McGee of West Bromwich Albion played out of position in a tactical ploy to stop Morton in 1925. He didn't succeed either. McGee was to say, "I could catch him all right – except that I never knew which way he was going." The *Daily Mail* made the comment, "The little man from Rangers with his magical feet led 'Policeman McGee' a merry dance." No defender England picked in a decade could master him.

The Sassenachs had to suffer the Rangers winger in every year but one from 1921 to 1932. He also played in almost all of the Scottish League versus Football League fixtures in that era. He was the terror of the English and was christened by journalist Ivan Sharpe as the 'Wee Blue

Alan Morton, a Rangers and Scotland idol and the terror of the English.

Devil' after completely bamboozling an English defence in one stunning display. Sharpe had overheard an English fan speaking with a broad Lancastrian accent the frustrated words, "Yon little blue devil." The nickname stuck.

Morton became the first name Scotland's selectors wrote on to their team-sheet during the years between the wars. He broke the record for international appearances in 1932 when he topped 30 games in the England versus Scotland meeting at Wembley. All told, Alan's 31 games stood as a record until fellow Ranger George Young passed it during the Fifties.

Morton was initially selected for Scotland during the celebratory Victory Internationals of 1919. An amateur with Queen's Park, he had been picked for an unofficial England-Scotland meeting in aid of war funds a year earlier, and then in February 1919 played for the Scottish League against the Football League at St Andrews, Birmingham. The following month he was in the full Scotland side that met Ireland, at Ibrox, and then appeared in the double meeting with the English where he greatly impressed the selectors ... and started his personal rout of England. At Goodison Park, he made Scotland's two goals in a 2-2 draw with precision crosses, and at Hampden Park, although Scotland lost 4-3, Morton netted a fine goal.

International football returned to normality in season 1919/20 and Alan Morton won his first official cap against Wales at Ninian Park, Cardiff. Scotland drew 1-1, a poor performance, but one report noted Morton as the "shining star". He soon became an automatic choice in Scotland's blue, quickly overshadowing Dundee's Alec Troup who was an early rival.

Alan scored in his next match against Ireland, then missed the Auld Enemy clash due to injury, but in the following season – by this time featuring as a hero with Rangers – he starred at Hampden Park against England, scoring with a spectacular shot-cum-centre in the first minute of the second half. He was called by one newspaper a "wonder juggler" in that 3-0 Scotland victory.

He continued to make headlines for Scotland, reaping acclaim in almost every international. In 1924 he was one of the Scots XI who played at Wembley for the first time. Eminent soccer writer Geoffrey Green noted in his recollection of that match: "What lives on in faded memory was the artistry of Scotland's immortal left-winger Alan Morton." Against Ireland in 1927, Alan scored both goals in a 2-0 victory and, by the time the clash with England was due to be played at the end of March 1928 and the Wembley Wizards were born, Morton was 34 years of age. He was the oldest member of the side, yet, remarkably, the Scot played on with fervour and zest. He continued at the top level of football until he was 40, allowing experience and cunning to substitute for pace when age finally caught up with him.

As a Wembley Wizard, Morton had England in a maze, creating three of Scotland's goals in the spree. He was always a big occasion footballer who loved the atmosphere generated at Wembley or Hampden Park. In Scotland's forward line he was a complete contrast to Jackson, Dunn, Gallacher and James, four colourful personalities. Morton was a model professional, who rarely lost his temper, even when the victim of much physical attention by frustrated defenders fed up with his dummies and switching of the ball from foot to foot. He was a gentleman of the old school and referees were untroubled by him, a player who scorned revenge through illegal means, unlike his lively colleagues. Morton would always concentrate on abstracting punishment for a hefty tackle by football alone. He would take the ball up to his full-back, weave one way, go to the other side almost contemptuously, and clip a "Morton lob", as it was to be known, into the penalty area – a perfect balloon high cross in front of the bar that goalkeepers and centre-halves hated, and when it dipped viciously, centre-forwards loved.

It was skill learned the hard way. Morton was not what could be called a natural born footballer. One of five sons of a coal engineer, he was born in the Jordanhill district of Glasgow in 1893 but was reared in Airdrie.

As a schoolboy he practised for hours a day with a small ball, "until I felt I was the master of it". The longer he was left alone to tap it against his coal-cellar door and yard wall the happier he was. Day after day the youngster practised, especially with his wrong left foot, aiming for a hole in the door and hitting the rebound no matter how difficult the angle was. It was practice that served him well in the future and an inspiration to all youngsters. Morton once described how he became a good player. "The three essentials are balance, ball control and quickness off the mark. They can only come from intensive practice, practice mark you, that was never a labour but a love, it gave me confident use of both feet . . . proficiency came slowly but in a way that became natural the longer I kept at it. At first, it was all deliberate, but later it became almost automatic." Morton was a player who thought about the game intensely. He even decided to wear only three studs in his boots, one at the toe and the other two further up the sole, an idea which enabled him to pivot more quickly.

At Airdrie Academy, Alan won school medals and in 1910 played for the Rest of Scotland XI against Glasgow. In youth football more success followed and he won Stirling Juvenile Cup and Ayrshire Charity Cup honours. It was clear that Morton would have a career in the game.

As well as having a love for football, Morton followed his father into the mining business. He trained as an engineer, a profession Alan remarkably doubled with throughout his football days. He was to work during the day, train in the evening, many times alone, and star in front of thousands on a Saturday. Oddly, he rarely practised with his Rangers team-mates, yet fitted into the unit without any trouble. He even on occasion worked the morning of a big match before casually strolling to the ground to swop his briefcase for football boots.

His elder brother, Robert, played in the same youth sides, and the pair were soon drawing the attention of Scottish League clubs. Airdrie manager John Chapman asked Alan to play in a trial, in a benefit game at Broomfield Park. The Airdrieonians were young Morton's favourite team and he longed to play for the Diamonds. However the Airdrie boss handed Alan the centre-forward's shirt, a role he had played but did not favour, for the game against Motherwell. Although he scored, Airdrie never asked him to sign forms, much to Alan's disappointment.

Queen's Park were the next club to become aware of the name Morton. Both Alan and Bob were invited to the Glasgow club and were soon in their reserve XI. The brothers signed for the Hampden outfit, a truly amateur club, and Scotland's oldest, just before the outbreak of World War One, in 1913. Queen's suited Alan, with their religious upholding of amateur traditions. He could continue his training as an engineer without interruption or conflict of interests. In those days Queen's Park players still had to provide their own strip. They even had to wash it too.

Before war started Alan appeared in the Scottish League for the first time. He soon impressed his club's committee with a glorious goal on his début against Third Lanark in November 1913, a goal past one of Scotland's best goalkeepers, Jimmy Brownlie, in a 2-2 draw. He played 27 games in his first season and had established a place on the left-wing. His brother also did well, earning the centre-forward shirt. Queen's Park, though, found it hard in Division One. Up against full-time professionals they continually struggled, finishing in 16th place in Morton's inaugural year.

During wartime football, the side's fortunes improved rapidly, with Morton becoming a star player in the black 'n' white hooped shirt. Three years on, in 1917/18, their progress was such that Queen's occupied seventh place; never before had they reached such a high position. *All Sports Weekly* was impressed with their line-up and noted at the time: "Queen's Park continue to win matches in a manner that has aroused intense enthusiasm in the West of Scotland, where their magnificent fight to keep amateurism to the fore has rallied all sections of the public to their support."

Queen's Park, however, always found it difficult to keep quality players. They had little hope of stopping a professional club poaching talented individuals once interest had been aroused. There were no contracts and a player could move on easily. It was to nobody's surprise when Alan Morton made the move after seven seasons of playing for nothing. He had already become a Scotland player and was much coveted by another Glasgow club.

His reputation had grown immensely and it was Scotland's top side, League Champions Rangers who were determined to take him to Ibrox Park as a replacement for another Scottish legend, Alex Smith. In June 1920 a deal was concluded after a series of negotiations. As an amateur Morton conducted his own bargaining. One of the best ways for a footballer to make money in those days was to turn professional as the player, rather than his club, was able to keep any transfer fee. Morton was a big enough star to command a large fee. It was reported that £3,000 was agreed, even £4,000, converted into an additional weekly wage for the player, said to be as high as £50 per week. It was a lucrative move for the winger then reputed to be the highest-paid player in Britain. Additionally he agreed with Rangers' management that he could keep his full-time job – he was now a fully qualified mining engineer.

The opening of the 1920s marked a decisive switch in the dominance of Scottish football with Rangers replacing their Old Firm rivals, Celtic, the club who had reigned supreme in pre-war days. The Ibrox side were to ascend for almost the next 20 years. Up to the Second World War the Light Blues won no fewer than 15 of the 20 Championships and reached

Queen's Park during the First World War in 1917, including the Morton brothers. Back row, left to right: Nelson, Ward, Strang (secretary). Middle row: Nutt (trainer), Aitken, Inglis, Wilson (trainer), Duncan, Ford, Hillhouse, Young. Front row: Mackenzie, Morton (Robert), Cowan, White (President), Morton (Alan), Paton, Stevenson.

nine Cup finals. Four times they won the double. Alan Morton was to figure in an important role, firstly as a player, then as director.

The former Queen's Park man was Willie Struth's first signing as manager of Rangers. Struth had been appointed after the tragic death of William Wilton who was drowned in a freak accident near Gourock. Struth possessed a magical influence. He was in charge until 1953, thought to be the longest period as a boss at any club.

Immediately Morton tasted success, although for the first couple of months he could not find any sort of form and some critics complained that Rangers had signed a failure. But after he had settled down, Rangers regained the Championship in 1920/21 in marvellous style. They only lost once in the 42-match programme, to Celtic of all teams, on New Year's Day. It was a League record and their 76 points had established another feat too. Celtic were runners-up . . . a massive ten points behind.

Morton started a highly productive liaison with inside colleague Tommy

Cairns, a partnership that was a dominant influence on the 'Gers' success. Cairns, well-built and "rough hewn from Scottish mines", as Morton once remarked, was an ideal foil to the delicate touch of the outside-left. The pair also appeared for Scotland together on several occasions.

Rangers reached the Scottish Cup final in 1921, meeting Partick Thistle, Jimmy McMullan's side. The Firhill club shocked Rangers and the rest of Scotland by winning 1-0, one of a series of bewildering results for Morton's team in the Scottish Cup, something of a hoodoo competition for the Ibrox club. They reached the final again 12 months later, and again fell to lesser opposition, this time to Greenock Morton, a team that had been toppled convincingly in home and away League meetings. Rangers paid the price for underestimating the opposition and despite a good personal performance by Alan Morton – he hit the post and had a shot kicked off the line – Rangers' Scottish Cup jinx continued. The Cappielaw side went on to win the Cup and were as surprised as anyone at lifting the trophy. They even had to borrow the celebration champagne that had been left in Rangers' dressing-room!

It had been a disappointing season for Ibrox spectators, as Celtic had also pipped the 'Gers for the title by one point. But Alan Morton and the rest of Struth's side were to make amends. Rangers went on to win a hat-trick of championships in 1923, 1924 and 1925, in each year heading off the challenge of Airdrie. Apart from Morton and Cairns, the Ibrox side was packed with other notable players, many of them long servants to the club like Morton. Dave Meiklejohn was captain and a huge inspiration, Bert Manderson and Billy McCandless, two talented full-backs. Andy Cunningham was an elegant schemer and Sandy Archibald a hefty but effective winger. In goal, Tom Hamilton was a tall and strong custodian while Tully Craig, a left-half of attacking qualities, was a Wembley Wizard reserve. Arthur Dixon was another yeoman Ranger and Tom Muirhead a great attacking half-back and utility player. It was a remarkable array of talent that performed consistently over a long period of time. As one star retired or moved on, another formidable personality stepped in without disrupting the team's style or performance.

Although Rangers dominated the League scene, their enigma in Cup football continued. In 1922/23 they were knocked out early on by Ayr United, the following year by Hibernian and in 1924/25 suffered a humiliating 5-0 semi-final defeat at the hands of Celtic. The next two years were to be little better, with the Ibrox side going out to St Mirren and Falkirk. 1928, though, was to be at last Rangers', and Alan Morton's, turn to win the elusive Scottish Cup.

Rangers emerged from a Cup wilderness. They had not lifted the trophy since 1903 – 25 long years without success. After a convincing

Alan Morton greets G.N. Foster at a meeting of Queen's Park and the Corinthians.

*With Rangers, Alan won trophy after trophy as the Ibrox club went through their greatest
ever period.*

route to the semi-final via opponents East Stirlingshire, King's Park and
Albion Rovers, they met Hibernian at Tynecastle. Jimmy Dunn was in
the Hibee side but goals from Archibald, McPhail and Simpson took
the Govan men into the final to meet great rivals Celtic, the team that
had thrashed Rangers in the semi-final three years previously, a defeat
Rangers' fans found very hard to come to terms with.

Celtic were holders and were contesting their fourth successive final.
It was the first Old Firm final since 1909 and 118,115 crowded into
Hampden Park to see the spectacle on a sunny day in April. It was
a record crowd for any domestic match up to then and they saw Alan
Morton play an important part in the crucial opening goal after a scoreless
first-half. The Rangers winger flashed down the left by-line, clipped
over a penetrating cross that reached Jimmy Fleming and, with the ball
heading for the net, Celtic skipper Willie McStay stopped a certain goal
with his hand . . . a clear penalty. Davie Meiklejohn crashed the spot-kick
home and Rangers were on their way. Morton teased Celtic's defenders
all afternoon and made the Blues' spectators roar with joy. More goals
followed as Rangers avenged their semi-final defeat. Bob McPhail netted
and Sandy Archibald hit the target with two superb shots to make the final
scoreline 4-0.

The Scottish Cup crowned a marvellous season. Alan Morton went on
to another League Championship medal, his sixth up to then, seven days
after the Hampden victory. It was Rangers' first ever double and the start
of an even better period than had just passed, as if the previous eight years

Morton was a regular for Scotland until he was almost 40.

had not been good enough. From 1928 to the outbreak of the Second World War, Rangers won the Championship trophy on nine occasions and the Scottish Cup six times. They also dominated both the Glasgow Cup and the Charity Cup. It was to be an era known as 'Eleven Great Years', the finest period in the history of the club.

Although Alan Morton was now well into his thirties he remained a regular for both Rangers and Scotland. Morton always kept himself in prime condition, as fit as any younger colleague. Inside Ibrox he was known as the 'Wee Society Man', immaculately dressed with suit, tie, bowler and, often, leather gloves and an umbrella. His hair would always be gleaming black, with a neat, almost perfect, parting. He was tidy on the soccer field too. Socks were neatly rolled up, shirt inside the shorts and boots always polished. His attitudes and disciplines were exactly what Rangers' Football Club and boss Struth aimed for – good presentation and gentlemanly conduct both on and off the field.

Tributes to the man's playing ability were always of the very highest order. Sir Frederick Wall, for long secretary of the English Football Association, wrote about Morton, the menace of his nation. He noted that Morton was "most dexterous as a dribbler . . . helped by the elusiveness of his small body, which he could swerve like a schoolmaster's cane". The senior administrator also said, "His brain was quick to see the situation and his feet swiftly adept at working it out." Rangers colleague Bob McPhail, the man who replaced Tommy Cairns as Morton's partner, once noted that Alan was "simply, in a class by himself", while Hughie Gallacher wrote in his memoirs "the best left-winger I have seen, all his reflexes seemed to co-ordinate perfectly".

Morton always went forward in a direct way . . . in a straight line for goal more often than not. He knew all the tricks all right but tended to leave the intricacies of wing play to others. He rarely headed the ball but frequently found the net. Above all he was consistent, week after week, year after year, and remained enthusiastic for the game.

In 1929 Rangers won the Championship, but lost in the Scottish Cup final again, this time to Kilmarnock. However, they created a remarkable record of clocking up 45 League and Cup games without defeat, over 12 months of football. Few could stop the 'Gers' machine. They won the double once again the following year, though Morton missed the first Cup final meeting at Hampden Park against Partick Thistle due to an injury picked up in the international meeting with England. Rangers were well below their best in a goalless draw and Morton returned for the replay the following Wednesday, again at Hampden. However, he had to hobble to the touchline after only 15 minutes of the game and took little part in the tussle thereafter. Even with ten men Rangers made sure their ageing maestro added another Cup medal to his collection by winning the replay 2-1. In that 1929/30 season Alan received a Grand Slam of medals as Rangers lifted everything; the Championship, the Cup, the Glasgow Cup and the Charity Cup. Even the club's reserve side won the Second XI Cup and Alliance Championship . . . they won every major honour in the Scottish game.

International players walked the corridors of Ibrox in numbers that were the envy of every club in Scotland. In 1931 no fewer than 13 capped players were at the club. Men to come into the side included James Marshall, a doctor by profession and a great character at inside-forward, Jimmy Fleming, a leader with a prolific scoring record, and Dougie Gray,

On retirement Morton became a director of Rangers and was associated with the Blues until his death in 1971.

who played almost 900 games for Rangers. Jock Buchanan, ex-Morton and St Mirren, was there and wing-half George Brown, to become another legend, entered the action as Morton reached the veteran stage. So did centre-half Jimmy Simpson and Jerry Dawson, a noted goalkeeper.

Season 1930/31 was Alan Morton's last as a regular in the Blues' line-up, a season in which he also skippered Scotland for the first and only time, in a game against Ireland. Rangers won the title again, their fifth success in a row, by toppling East Fife on the last day of the season. Alan was in and out of the side the following year but, at 39 years of age, was still good enough to appear for the Scots' national side, albeit his last appearance in his country's jersey. He became the oldest ever to play for Scotland and one of the oldest of all time for any country. Morton played in three fixtures of the season – against Wales, against England, when he broke Scotland's appearance record, and lastly in May 1932 against France in Paris. He ended on a winning note, the Scots cruising to a 3-1 victory thanks largely to Morton's expertise on the wing and a Neil Dewar hat-trick.

Morton's final match for Rangers came during the 1932/33 season, another year the Championship ended up in Govan. He had appeared in a total of 598 League fixtures in a truly outstanding career. Only Motherwell's Bobby Ferrier (626 games) can boast a better Scottish League record. All told, Alan totalled over 700 senior games and scored 151 goals spanning 20 seasons. Nine Championship medals came his way and he appeared in five Cup finals. In all those years Alan never played for Rangers' second XI.

His days with Rangers Football Club were far from over. On retirement he was quickly elevated to a director at Ibrox. It is something of a rarity in football for a player to reach that status, although Rangers are an exception. Up to the recent installation of Graeme Souness as a director, the Ibrox club have appointed several ex-stars to the boardroom, and in a highly successful way. Alan brought his vast football knowledge to the administrative side of the club and helped the Blues continue along the same successful lines as when he was a player.

For almost 40 years Morton remained in Rangers' upper management. He witnessed many changes in the game at first hand during the years up to his retirement in June 1971. He resigned due to ill health and was confined to a wheelchair in his later years.

A bachelor all his life, Alan Morton died at his home in Airdrie six months later, in December 1971, when 78 years of age. It was on the same day another ex-Rangers forward passed away – Torry Gillick. A minute's silence was observed in Alan Morton's honour at the Rangers versus Airdrie fixture the following weekend.

The *Glasgow Herald* noted that Morton was "one of the greatest footballers of his generation". He created an everlasting picture of the perfect footballer, perhaps the most famous Ranger of all time. Ibrox still holds Alan Morton in special esteem and his portrait is prominently placed in the club's hallway.

Those who saw him were lucky indeed. They were entranced at the grace of the little man. Now all most of us can do is imagine. As one contemporary report described the Morton genius, "He wriggles down the wing with a mesmerising shimmy shake which leaves his opponents stone cold." No doubt a wicked cross followed and the ball ended bulging the net. Another goal courtesy of the Morton lob.

ALAN LAUDER MORTON

Career Span: 1913 to 1933
Born: Jordanhill, Glasgow, 24 April 1893
Died: Airdrie, 15 December 1971
Career: Queen's Park, 1913; Rangers, 1920, becoming a director in 1933 to his retirement in 1971
Club Honours:
Scottish League Championship 1921, 1923, 1924, 1925, 1927, 1928, 1929, 1930, 1931
Scottish Cup winner 1928, 1930
Scottish Cup runner-up 1921, 1922, 1929
Scottish League runner-up 1922, 1932
Full Internationals: 31 appearances, five goals, 1920-32
1919/20 v Wales, Ireland (1)
1920/21 v England (1)
1921/22 v Wales, England
1922/23 v Ireland, Wales, England
1923/24 v Wales, N. Ireland, England
1924/25 v Wales, N Ireland, England
1926/27 v N Ireland (2), England (1)
1927/28 v Wales, N Ireland, England
1928/29 v Wales, N Ireland, England
1929/30 v Wales, N Ireland, England
1930/31 v Wales, N Ireland, England
1931/32 v Wales, England, France
Victory Internationals: Three appearances, one goal, 1919.
1918/19 v England, England (1), Ireland
War Internationals: One appearance, no goals, 1918
1917/18 v England
Scottish League XI: 15 appearances, one goal, 1919-32
1918/19 v Football League, Football League
1919/20 v Football League, Irish League
1920/21 v Football League
1921/22 v Football League
1922/23 v Football League
1923/24 v Football League (1)
1924/25 v Football League, Irish League
1925/26 v Football League
1926/27 v Football League
1928/29 v Football League
1929/30 v Football League
1931/32 v Football League

MATCH ANALYSIS

Season	Club	League app-gls	Cup app-gls	Scotland app-gls	Other represent- ative app-gls	Total app-gls
1913-14	Queen's Park (Div 1)	22-4	5-0	—	—	27-4
1914-15	Queen's Park (Div 1)	37-4	—	—	—	37-4
1915-16	Queen's Park (Div 1)	38-8	—	—	—	38-8
1916-17	Queen's Park (Div 1)	38-6	—	—	—	38-6
1917-18	Queen's Park (Div 1)	33-14	—	—	1-0	34-14
1918-19	Queen's Park (Div 1)	24-3	—	—	5-1	29-4
1919-20	Queen's Park (Div 1)	26-7	3-1	2-1	2-0	33-9
1920-21	Rangers (Div 1)	39-6	6-1	1-1	1-0	47-8
1921-22	Rangers (Div 1)	30-4	8-3	2-0	1-0	41-7
1922-23	Rangers (Div 1)	35-3	2-1	3-0	1-0	41-4
1923-24	Rangers (Div 1)	34-6	3-0	3-0	1-1	41-7
1924-25	Rangers (Div 1)	36-8	5-0	3-0	2-0	46-8
1925-26	Rangers (Div 1)	29-5	5-0	—	1-0	35-5
1926-27	Rangers (Div 1)	31-10	5-4	2-3	1-0	39-17
1927-28	Rangers (Div 1)	34-11	6-2	3-0	—	43-13
1928-29	Rangers (Div 1)	37-13	6-4	3-0	1-0	47-17
1929-30	Rangers (Div 1)	24-5	7-0	3-0	1-0	35-5
1930-31	Rangers (Div 1)	32-7	2-1	3-0	—	37-8
1931-32	Rangers (Div 1)	13-0	3-0	3-0	1-0	20-0
1932-33	Rangers (Div 1)	6-3	—	—	—	6-3
Total		598-127	66-17	31-5	19-2	714-151

*Morton additionally appeared in 78 other senior fixtures scoring over 20 goals, for both Queen's Park and Rangers, in matches in the Glasgow Charity Cup, Glasgow Cup and Victory Cup.

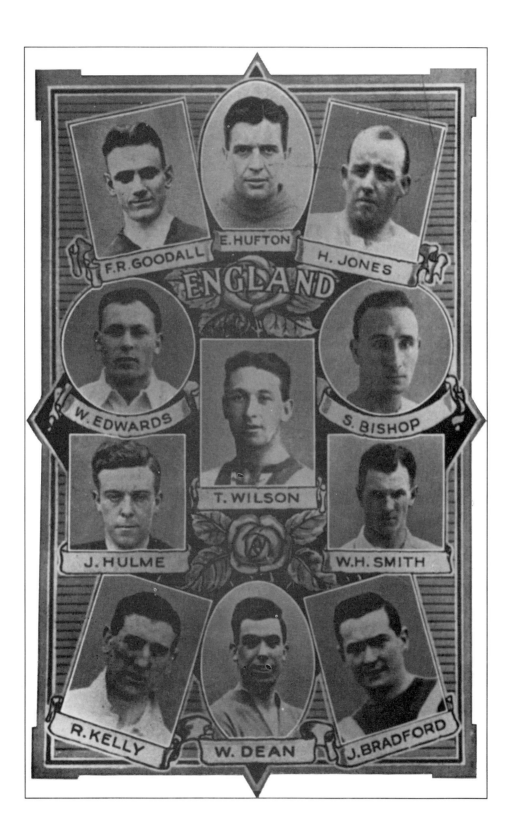

ENGLAND

F.R. GOODALL   E. HUFTON   H. JONES

W. EDWARDS   S. BISHOP

T. WILSON

J. HULME   W.H. SMITH

R. KELLY   W. DEAN   J. BRADFORD

14

ELEVEN SASSENACHS

The English defence as a whole, will take a lot of penetrating.
The Times, March 1928

IN THE previous season's international matches of 1926/27 England had a formidable record. They were unbeaten having played six games, winning four and scoring an impressive 28 goals. It was a far better record than Scotland's performances. They had fallen 2-1 to the English at Hampden Park in front of 111,214 fans, in a game in which débutants Hulme and Jones did well and captain Roy Goodall was outstanding. Dixie Dean cracked home two late goals which gave England their first win in Scotland for all of 23 years and spoiled the home country's run of nine wins and a draw in the last ten matches, the last seven won without conceding a goal.

England had drawn with both Ireland and Wales but went goal-crazy on a mini-tour of Europe. They thrashed Belgium 9-1, defeated Luxembourg 5-2, then gave France a 6-0 hiding. Dean grabbed eight goals in the romp. There was a feeling in the English camp that they had a reasonably settled side and had put together a combination to be feared. Much was expected from the Sassenachs for the following 1927/28 season.

Up till then, the years after World War One had been nothing short of a disaster for English international football. They rarely had a regular line-up, only twice did they field the same 11 players in consecutive games, and that on tour. Changes were made for virtually every one of the 49 fixtures during the Twenties. Scotland held superiority over them in the showpiece of the year, the Saxons, as England were then commonly referred to by Scots journalists, winning only two meetings up to 1928. England would have to wait until 1930 to lift the Home International Championship outright – 17 years since they last could be called the best in Britain.

This poor state of affairs, however, was all behind them and almost forgotten when the new international season kicked off in October 1927. Such was the transformation in England's side – or so everyone thought. They travelled to Belfast to meet Northern Ireland and far from looking like a team that was at last to win the championship, they failed miserably. The Irish won 2-0 through a goal by Mahood and an own-goal by left-back Jones. Changes were made for the following month's encounter with Wales at Turf Moor, Burnley, but it mattered little as England lost again, this time 2-1. Even England's goal was scored by a Welshman, Fred Keenor putting through his own net.

Ted Hufton, goalkeeper of West Ham United, and the best in the world according to many.

Fans and media were furious at the side's display. Criticism was thrown from every angle at the players and selectors. By the time the clash with Scotland at Wembley drew near later in the season, England's team was the subject of much discussion. Changes had to be made. In fact in the three games of the year 20 different players were used. Débuts had been given to goalkeeper Tremelling and to Cooper and Nuttall, while Osborne, Baker and Ball, team-mate of Tom Bradshaw at Bury, were given opportunities too. Several players were recalled for only their second games, including Hutton, Earle and Storer. It had been an inexperienced and unsettled outfit. But with further changes England still felt confident that they could pick up the pieces with a win over the Scots. After all, Scotland had fared a little better, losing also to Ireland and ending level with Wales. The Football Association's selectors were to choose, on paper anyway, a competent looking line-up for the Wembley clash in March.

They met at Everton's offices at Goodison Park and announced a side that rendered good press comment. *The Times* noted, "The English defence as a whole, will take a lot of penetrating", while a Scottish viewpoint was made by *The Bulletin*: "It is a good side, probably too robust in the rear and strong at wing-half for Scotland's attack." Not that England's side escaped some diverse reaction. The side contained five players, which ended up as six after illness robbed England of their captain, Bishop, who had a very good chance of playing in the FA Cup final due to be played after the England v Scotland meeting.

Roy Goodall, one of Huddersfield Town's array of talent in the 1928 England/Scotland meeting.

Blackburn Rovers were already through to the final while Huddersfield Town were involved in a torrid series of replays with Sheffield United. It was noted that Cup nerves would perhaps affect performances for England, although Scotland had similar hypothetical worries with Alec Jackson and Alan Morton also in Cup thrills, not to mention McMullan, who was at the end of a promotion push with Manchester City.

England's back four of goalkeeper Ted Hufton, backs Roy Goodall and Bert Jones, together with centre-half Tom Wilson looked a strong unit. West Ham United's Hufton had received the nod over Dan Tremelling of Birmingham City, both having made only a handful of appearances for their country. Hufton had built a huge reputation in the south, so

Blackburn Rovers in 1927/28, featuring both Harry Healless and Bert Jones. Jones is second from the right in the back row, Healless is sitting in the front row with the ball, Rovers' captain.

big that he was dubbed the "best in the world" by some. He was a crowd personality and pleased spectators with a string of spectacular saves. He was as brave as they come, noted for diving fearlessly at the feet of onrushing forwards. Hufton, a Nottinghamshire man, started with Sheffield United just before the war and was wounded while serving with the Coldstream Guards in France. Afterwards he joined West Ham and went on to appear in over 400 games for the Hammers, including the famous White Horse Cup final, the first at Wembley in 1923. All told he won six caps for England.

Roy Goodall and Bert Jones represented two of the strongest teams in the Football League that season, Huddersfield Town and Blackburn Rovers. The pair had formed a settled partnership for the national side during two seasons, unusually so for England at that time. Their combination had looked solid in the Inter-League challenge match three weeks before when Scotland were given a soccer lesson.

Huddersfield Town had just won a treble of League Championships and they had no fewer than four players in England's side. Apart from Goodall and Wilson, Kelly and Smith also came from Leeds Road, as did Scotland's Alec Jackson of course. Huddersfield were the team of

Tom Wilson, winning his first cap at centre-half.

the age and Roy Goodall played an important role in their success. He was England captain, deputising for Sid Bishop, and a highly respected professional who, Alan Morton was to note, "always impressed me". Goodall was never overawed by a big occasion and he had been through plenty of those since joining Huddersfield in 1921. He was fast and believed in giving his opposing winger a tough match, frequently using the shoulder charge. The Yorkshireman was an England regular over a long period, winning 25 caps, and was later associated with Nottingham Forest, Mansfield Town and Huddersfield in managerial capacities.

Goodall's partner, Bert Jones, was part of a Blackburn Rovers team that had reached the FA Cup final in 1928. Also in the England side was a further Rovers star, Harry Healless. Jones was another who could be regarded as fleet of foot. He was dauntless and a master of positional awareness. From Blackpool, Bert started with his home club before joining Blackburn in 1925, ending his career with Brighton in the late Thirties. Between 1927 and 1928 he was at his peak and won all of his six honours for England then.

Another Huddersfield player in England's defence was Tom Wilson who was to make his début – and as it turned out, only, appearance – in the match with Scotland. He was a robust centre-half who possessed outstanding heading ability and who was the anchor-man of the Leeds Road club's success that brought them three titles and saw them reach four Cup finals. From Seaham in County Durham, Wilson was overshadowed in the England side by Jack Hill for a long period, but had at last been given his chance in the national white shirt. Since Wilson's League baptism with the Terriers in 1919, it was evident that he was an immensely talented half-back who, like Tom Bradshaw had changed from an attack-minded role into a stopper centre-half.

Willis Edwards of Second Division Leeds United. A stylish midfielder.

Despite the glowing press reports of the selection and undoubted status of England's defence, they, Hufton expected, were to have a harrowing 90 minutes as they faced Scotland's forwards on dazzling form.

The only Second Division player in England's ranks was right-half Willis Edwards of Leeds United. Although he was at the time in Division Two, his club's stay in the second grade was to be a brief one. Leeds had been relegated in 1927 but were back up in the same year as the Wizards' match, promoted along with Jimmy McMullan and Manchester City. Edwards was a half-back for the connoisseur and won 16 caps between 1926 and 1930, practically everpresent for England. He was a delight to watch. He possessed wonderful ball control and had the ability to collect a ball and hit a pass to win a game. Edwards was brought up in the coal-mining area of Derbyshire and made his League début when 17 years of age, with Chesterfield. He joined Leeds in 1925, the start of over 35 years at Elland Road as player, trainer and manager.

The second link between defence and attack was Harry Healless who played for England only twice. He stepped into the side as a last-minute replacement for Leicester City's Sid Bishop who withdrew because of stomach trouble only a day before the match was to be played. Healless was an experienced club player with Blackburn Rovers, versatile and consistent, and he was skipper of the Ewood Club. However, he was pushed into England's line-up out of position, taking the left-half spot instead of his normal right-sided role. A dour performer, Healless had a relentless tackle and spent all of his footballing days with Rovers, in the town of Blackburn where he had been born and bred.

England's forwards, led by the personality of the moment, Dixie Dean, looked awesome. Bob Kelly and Joe Bradford were inside men who could score goals, and on the flanks Joe Hulme and Billy Smith

Joe Bradford, Birmingham City's goalscoring inside-forward.

were, according to England's faithful, every bit as good as Morton and Jackson.

Kelly and Bradford had the all-important function at inside-forward of making England's front line tick. The much-travelled Bob Kelly wore the inside-right shirt. Lancashire-born, he started with Burnley, winning a Championship medal there in 1921, then moved to Sunderland for a record fee four years later. He was transferred to Huddersfield in 1927 and after a good spell in their star-studded team moved on to Preston and into management with both Carlisle and Stockport. Kelly was one of the greatest names between the wars, although always in and out of the England side. He won 14 caps and could call upon wonderful ball control and remarkable acceleration over a short distance.

Joe Bradford of Birmingham City was another who was quick off the mark. At home at either inside- or centre-forward, he was a deadly marksman and once scored five goals in a single match for the Football League. He proved a more than useful inside-left, always liable to grab goals. At St Andrews he netted a record 267 over 15 years. Bradford helped Birmingham to win the Second Division championship and scored in their Cup final appearance in 1931. He played for his country on 12 occasions.

In 1928 Arsenal had not yet become the force they were to be in the Thirties decade, but several of the players to take leading roles in that period of glory were making their names in football. Alex James was one, another was flying winger, Joe Hulme, known as the "Highbury Express". Scotland feared his speed – he was reputed to be the fastest man in the game – and he was to be England's danger man along with Dean. At Ibrox Park a matter of three weeks before, Hulme had showed Scotland what a menace he could be with a devastating display in the

Bob Kelly, a huge personality in England and team-mate of Alec Jackson.

Joe Hulme, a danger with his speed, one Scotland's defence had to watch closely.

Football League's 6-2 victory. He netted twice and gave full-back McStay an awful evening.

Before joining the Highbury staff, Hulme was briefly with York City and at Blackburn alongside Healless and Jones. Born in Stafford, he signed for Arsenal in 1926 and won everything with the Gunners, over and over again. He moved to Huddersfield in 1938 and went on to reach a fifth FA Cup final. Hulme possessed numerous tricks to beat his marker and was a regular choice for England during the Twenties until he lost his place to another speed machine, Sammy Crooks of Derby County. Hulme was also a fine cricketer, appearing for Middlesex over a ten-year period.

On the other touchline was Billy Smith, Huddersfield's celebrated outside-left. He was to the Yorkshire club as Alan Morton was to Rangers. Smith hardly missed a game in the Terriers' successful years and stayed with the club from 1913 to 1934, totalling 572 games for the Leeds Road side. Another in England's ranks from County Durham, Smith was long-legged and produced an unusual loping manner when in full stride. It was an unusual style, but one that weaved a magic spell up and down the left flank in an elusive way hard for defenders to cope with. He was a good goalscorer too, and he and Alec Jackson in Huddersfield's side were a deadly combination feared on every ground in the Football League. Although Smith was rated as among the very best at club level, English selectors preferred his rivals, notably Burnley's Louis Page and Jimmy Ruffell of West Ham, much to the annoyance of many involved in the game. Billy won only three caps.

The man England relied on more than any other was William Ralph Dean; big, strong and dashing in the leader's role. Until Dixie Dean had

Billy Smith, another threat on the wing.

Dixie Dean, England's spearhead, fresh from a record-breaking goal burst.

burst on to the international scene in 1927, the centre-forward position had been a problem one for England with almost 20 different Number 9s tried and discarded. Dean was first capped against Wales. He scored twice and became an immediate automatic choice. He had appeared in only seven fixtures up to the Wizards' match but had put 12 goals in the net for England. As the match at Wembley approached, Dean was completing an amazing season for his club, Everton, smashing the goalscoring record by whacking home 60 goals – 82 in all games – as the Goodison club lifted the title. His remarkable total remains a record to this day.

Dean was Merseyside-born and joined Everton from Tranmere Rovers in 1925. He could shoot powerfully, bustled up front and above all was a great exponent in the air. He had scored twice against the Scots League XI and found the net twice also in the last Auld Enemy international at Hampden Park. Tartan fans feared him more than anyone else. After winning 16 caps for England, Dean finished his career with Notts County and Sligo Rovers as war approached in 1939.

In the pre-match build up many thought England would have the edge. They had a more powerful, much taller and stronger line-up and were clear favourites to win the annual challenge. It was to be a contest between a big, burly but fast England team with aces Hulme, Smith and Dean, against the diminutive, dainty Scots with key stars Morton, James, Gallacher and Jackson. One writer who met some of England's party at their headquarters in Marylebone Road thought there would be an English walkover against what the *Sporting Chronicle* called "the lightest and smallest attack the land of the Thistle has ever had".

THE FOOTBALL ASSOCIATION

INTERNATIONAL MATCH

Stadium Wembley
March 31ST 1928

ENGLAND
v
SCOTLAND

The valve with the wonderful Mullard P.M. Filament.

Mullard
THE MASTER VALVE

OFFICIAL
PROGRAMME

PRICE
SIXPENCE

15

NINETY MINUTES OF MAGIC

To the skirl of the bagpipes Scotland caused the rose of England to wither and die at Wembley.
Sunday Chronicle, March 1928.

SATURDAY MORNING in London was dull, dreary and wet, but in the Scottish camp before the party left for the Empire Stadium, Jimmy McMullan was smirking, quietly confident and content. The evening before a few brief words had been spoken about the match. Robert Campbell, President of the Scottish FA, told skipper McMullan, "I think you'd better get your players upstairs now and talk about tomorrow's game."

The Scots captain was not one for great tactical discussion. He gathered his men on the first-floor landing and made a few remarks about conduct. "Now I don't want any unnecessary talking. Get on with the game and don't talk to opponents or the referee." He continued with the now famous words, "I think you all know as well as I do what's expected from you tomorrow. So get off to bed, put your head on the pillow and pray for rain." With such a light-weight forward line, a wet, treacherous surface would give the Scots a distinct advantage. They were small in stature, highly skilled on the ball and able to keep their balance on a slippery pitch far easier than their much bigger England markers.

London's weather on that day was to be perfectly suited to McMullan's team. In a year of atrocious weather, Friday saw thunderstorms accompanied by hail descend on the capital, but a strong wind quickly dried everything out. The forecast for Saturday, to McMullan's disappointment, was, "expected to be dry and fast". It was wrong. After a fine start the clouds opened and the lush Wembley turf became soaked through. McMullan's call was answered.

As kick-off approached it was still raining, lashing torrents on to the pitch. The weather did nothing to spoil the enthusiasm of the fans despite the fact that much of Wembley was then uncovered terracing and open to the elements. The gaiety of the crowd was infectious. Community singing with the band of the Irish Guards kept the growing masses occupied. A record attendance of 80,682, had gathered, the largest for any international in London up to then.

At a quarter to three the hollow thud of studs on the tiled corridors beneath the terracing could be heard by some. A *Pathe News* film crew waited. The players emerged from the tunnel to a deafening roar of welcome. The tartan army erupted as Jimmy McMullan led the Dark

Jimmy McMullan leads out the Wizards, followed by Alec Jackson, Hughie Gallacher and Jack Harkness.

The Duke of York meets Scotland's line-up. Left to right: *Dunn, Gallacher, Jackson, Gibson, Harkness, Nelson, Bradshaw.*

Blues out, flanked one by one with stand-in skipper, Roy Goodall, and England's side. The Englishmen towered over the Scottish XI.

Several Scots fans ran on to the field, a foretaste of the Sixties or Seventies era, to wish their heroes good luck. London bobbies frantically chased after them in comic style. The atmosphere was too much for many. Some of Scotland's inexperienced side were affected by the occasion – for several it was their first visit to Wembley. Young Jack Harkness, only 21-years-old then, was one who was initially overcome. He was nervous to the extreme and when looking up to the giant stadium thought that the flagpoles above the Wembley stands were revolving. The 'keeper was forced to grab hold of a goalpost to retain his balance and composure.

The Duke of York and his guest, King Amanullah of Afghanistan, were presented to the teams. The National Anthem played, without a Caledonian version, then referee Willie Bell took the stage. Bell, a native of Hamilton, was ready for the formalities. He called over his two linesmen, J.L. Morrison from Scotland and a certain S.F. Rous representing England. (Later, of course, he became Sir Stanley, President of FIFA.) The captains gathered, a few words of authority from Bell, a toss of the coin and the England versus Scotland meeting of 1928 was underway to a crescendo of noise.

Immediately Scotland were up against it as the game exploded into a thrilling start. England attacked from the kick-off. The ball went back into midfield and on to Bradford who swung a fine pass out to winger Billy Smith on the left touchline. The Huddersfield ace controlled the pass instantly and headed towards the Scottish penalty area. Full-back Nelson came up to face him. Smith feinted one way, Nelson lunged, slipped on the wet turf and was left sprawling as the winger went the opposite way. English fans roared with encouragement. Smith cut inside, went forward a few paces, aimed and fired in a left-footed drive from the edge of the box. Harkness rushed off his line to narrow the angle, made a desperate dive, but the ball flashed past his outstretched arm heading for the net. However, to the relief of the whole of Scotland, it struck the post and, with no England forward following up, the ball bounced to safety.

All of a minute or so of play had gone. Scotland had been given a lucky break. Had Billy Smith's early effort found the corner of the net instead of the woodwork, perhaps the legend of the Wembley Wizards would never have been born.

Within two minutes of that dramatic opening, play switched to the other end of the ground. It was Scotland's turn to threaten in a whirlwind start. McMullan collected the ball from defence. He shuffled forward, looked up and clipped the ball to Gibson. The Villa man found his inside colleague, Alex James, who in turn swept the ball to Gallacher and in one movement Scotland's leader pushed it out to Morton. Just as Smith

Referee William Bell and linesman Stanley Rous, then a Watford schoolmaster.

had done moments earlier, Morton dribbled to his full-back. The Rangers man went past Goodall on the outside and sent over a precision cross. In rushed Alec Jackson from the opposite flank to send a flashing header past Ted Hufton in the England goal and into the net. Scotland were 1-0 ahead in a remarkable opening. Hughie Gallacher said of the well-worked goal, "Not an England player touched the ball from the time Smith fired it against the Scottish woodwork." Alec Jackson had won his private bet with James as to who would score first; he would go on to win treble stakes too.

The slippery pitch saw defenders floundering just as McMullan had forecast, but it wasn't just England's men who had problems. Following that frenetic opening, Scotland appeared uneasy as England pressed for a quick equaliser. Hulme was menacing early on and the babe, Tommy Law, looked uncomfortable. Jack Harkness, though, proved to be England's equal. The amateur goalkeeper made good saves to keep Scotland ahead. He made a daring stop at the feet of three England forwards when a goal looked a certainty, then the Queen's Park man produced a marvellous double save. Dixie Dean, the sturdy Everton

Alex James fires home Scotland's second goal in the 44th minute. Goalkeeper Hufton has no chance.

leader, hit a strong shot from 35 yards which Harkness parried on his knees, then, with Bradford following up, Scotland's goalie dived again to save the day.

The men from the north weathered England's pressure and stuck to their close combination play with short passes to feet. Gradually Scotland took control of the game. Full-backs Law and Nelson overcame their opening nerves, Law held the thrusts of Hulme and Nelson subdued Smith, while Scotland's half-backs took a grip of midfield. Jimmy Gibson and Jimmy McMullan, once team-mates at Partick Thistle, began to dominate the field in front of their defence. They picked up all the loose balls and broke up England's advances. The home side's half-backs, Edwards and Healless, were only noticeable by their absence in the contest. It was to be the key battleground of the afternoon.

The midfield anchor-men in turn fed James and Dunn, and wingers Morton and Jackson, while at centre-forward Gallacher, in roving style, led his marker Tom Wilson a merry dance. Scotland's centre-forward was felled on two occasions just outside the box and Ted Hufton saved twice as Scotland threatened to increase their lead with shots by Jackson and Gibson. As the end of the first 45 minutes approached it looked like a 1-0 interval scoreline. However, just as the game started in dramatic fashion so the first half ended in similar circumstances.

The Royal Box. The Duke of York and guest, the King of Afghanistan, enjoy the confrontation.

With a minute remaining England had possession of the ball, with Billy Smith just inside his own half. The Huddersfield winger misplaced a pass straight to the feet of James. A quick move with Jimmy Gibson and Scotland were moving forward dangerously. James exchanged passes and Healless and Jones went out of the play. A one-two with Jackson, and, as Wilson came at him, James half turned and hit a low angled half-volley from the edge of the penalty box which left Hufton sprawling and the ball in the net for a superb effort. "A positively brilliant second goal," wrote *The Bulletin* correspondent. James noted, "I knew Ted Hufton would never get near it." Alex reckoned that was his greatest ever goal.

At half-time Scotland were 2-0 ahead, and the tartan fans, wet and bedraggled, sang out loud and clear and revelled in the atmosphere as though it was Hogmanay in Glasgow Cross or Edinburgh Tron. Scotland were perhaps flattered by the scoreline, but in the second period they gave a performance of colossal confidence. The *Daily Mail* commented, "Scotland's whole team played with a dominant mastery that was made to appear sheer effrontery," while another report noted, "They swept into attack again and again by beautiful dribbling and passing."

Scotland's front line went into scintillating action. Those diminutive forwards played a game suited to their ability and to the conditions;

concise passing in classic triangular moves up each wing. Gibson, Dunn and Jackson on the right, and McMullan, James and Morton on the left, with Gallacher creating space with intelligent running, "paving the way for other folks", as one reporter observed. Rarely did the ball go aimlessly in the air where the English defenders would have an advantage. It was, as the *Glasgow Herald* wrote, "as near perfection as is likely to be seen".

Early in the second-half Scotland went close several times and Alex James started to have a major influence on the match. Firstly, taking a pass from Jackson, he flashed a shot that thudded against the crossbar, then he tested Hufton with another blockbuster that the West Ham 'keeper saved well. Referee Bell turned down two strong Scottish penalty appeals when Gibson was up-ended in the 18-yard area and after Gallacher was also felled in the box.

Midfield became Scotland's domain the longer the game continued. Morton and Jackson were fed with the ball time and time again and England's full-backs Goodall and Jones couldn't find any way to stop the two wingers, with Jackson flying past his marker quicker on every trip. Another goal had to come – it did, 20 minutes from the restart.

Another delightful piece of half-back interplay found Morton on his customary by-line. Goodall was left on his backside as the Rangers' maestro pinpointed another telling cross into the danger area. The ball again found the head of Jackson who had lost his marker. With complete composure and accuracy he sent the ball sailing into the English net for another picture goal. A move almost identical to Scotland's opening effort.

Within a minute it was 4-0. From the restart Scotland totally demoralised the opposition with another stunning attack. Gallacher took the ball in close control and, head down, steamrollered towards the English penalty area weaving in and out of tackles. Bert Jones rushed in with a saving lunge on the edge of the box and sent Gallacher tumbling. The ball bounced free though . . . straight into the path of Alex James, who lashed the loose ball into the net off the outstretched body of Jones.

It was now a rout. Scotland toyed with their bulky and now lead-footed opponents and England deteriorated from bad to worse. The elusive wee Scots started to string moves of ten or more passes together and their fans cheered themselves hoarse at the sight of the English in complete disarray. They "roared with delight at the antics of James, chuckled with glee at the joyous swing of Jackson. Revelled in the Gallacher thrust", as one critic noted. The *Glasgow Herald* wrote that the Scots were "giving an all round exhibition of scientific football that was admittedly a revelation". They took and gave their passes at walking pace, underlining with rather cruel emphasis how much on top they were. By this time even the Cockneys in the crowd started to cheer the Scottish side.

Hughie Gallacher threatens.
Top: *Gallacher in a contest with Jones. Goodall and Wilson are watching.*
Bottom: *Gallacher shoots, watched by Goodall, Jones and Hufton.*

Alec Jackson rises to a Morton cross and scores Scotland's third goal. Gallacher and Dunn are in the picture, with Goodall of England.

As Scotland moved up a gear they started to pass the ball quickly between their forwards. To James, to Jackson, inside to Gallacher, back to McMullan and out to Morton. England's defenders frantically jumped in with desperate tackles but the greasy ball skidded past their clumsy lunges on to the next Scottish boot. The Dark Blues nipped in and out of the challenges one after another, releasing the ball just at the right moment. Their timing and anticipation was perfection. It was precision football at its very best.

Dean and Bradford slogged away at the other end of the field but, without midfield promptings or telling wing play, they were easy pickings for Tom Bradshaw in the centre of Scotland's defence. Harkness saved twice from counter attacks but the majority of any danger came at Hufton's goalmouth with Scotland's "Wee Blue Devils", as they were to be nicknamed, swarming round the England penalty box.

Ivan Sharpe in *Athletic News* superbly recorded Scotland's fifth goal, and the best of the afternoon. Five minutes from the end the ball was

Alec Jackson in full flight with Bert Jones, England's full-back looking on.

A section of Scottish support, pipes and all.

The England v Scotland clash featured football's most noted centre-forwards, Dixie Dean and Hughie Gallacher.

Dean (left) rarely got a look in but Gallacher (above) was a constant menace to England's defence, pictured giving 'keeper Hufton problems.

with midfield general Jimmy McMullan 40 yards from the England goal. Alan Morton was in space on the left. Sharpe wrote, "Jimmy! I heard the call for the ball pierce the noise. Morton, outside-left, called for a pass. No sooner said than done. Between half-back and full-back went the ball, like an arrow. Morton racing ahead in anticipation, caught it, eased up, crossed the ball a yard from the line, and as it fell in front of goal, Alex Jackson met it in the air three yards from the post and, crash! a volley-goal from point-blank range."

Poor Goodall was yet again left watching Morton's heels. Hufton had

Bob Kelly, he was England's best player and scored his country's consolation goal.

been caught in two minds with the wickedness of the cross and Jones was mesmerised as Jackson flashed past him. For the fifth time thousands of tartan tammies filled the sky. It was Jackson's hat-trick. He became the first man to score three goals at Wembley and one of only a handful of Scottish players to grab a trio against England, home or away. Modestly he was later to say, "I only had to hit them in." The service, all three crosses from Morton, was faultless and the finish deadly.

Jimmy McMullan mobbed by well-wishers after the final whistle.

Five-nil and it could have been much more. *The Times* observed, "Scotland by over indulgence in the pleasant pastime of making the English defence look supremely silly cheated themselves out of a sixth and possibly a seventh goal."

There was still time for another though, a consolation for England. In the final minute they were awarded a free-kick on the edge of the Scotland box. The goal was left to England's best player, Bob Kelly. When he had the ball – which was not often enough – England had a chance. He stepped up to wallop the free-kick straight into the net. The game, though, was by then well and truly over. Several minutes of injury time prolonged England's agony, with the cheeky Scots playing possession football – from one man to another, the ball went in teasing style.

Referee Bell was good enough to wait until a fellow Scot, Jack Harkness, had the ball, before blowing the final whistle. A magnificent 5-1 victory. Harkness grabbed the match-ball, stuffed it under his jersey and ran to the dressing-room. He later handed it to Scottish FA officials for safe keeping. The historic ball is now still preserved, suitably inscribed and autographed, in the trophy room at the Association's headquarters in Park Gardens, Glasgow.

Scotland's soaked followers were ecstatic. It had rained on and off throughout the match but no one cared about a drowning on that day. On the whistle McMullan and his men were engulfed by well-wishers. The Irish Guards came to life and played the Afghan national anthem, not a cheery tune, which perhaps caught the mood of England's men as they trooped away heads down.

It was a victory that had exceeded all the eternal optimistic hopes of the Scottish fans. And it wasn't just the margin of success, but the way in which the victory had been achieved. Nobody cared now about the defeat by the Irish, the thrashing by the Football League or the number of Anglos in the side. Everybody was a hero, a Scottish hero at that.

Press comment was sensational even in those somewhat reserved and tactfully reported times. Not since the very early days of the international fixture had a result been so emphatic.

DAILY MIRROR
"England were not beaten at Wembley. They were routed and outpaced by Scotland and thrashed by 5-1. And the wonder is that the score was not bigger."

DAILY MAIL
"In the annals of international football I do not think there is a parallel to this match."

SUNDAY CHRONICLE
"Never was a country more humiliated on its own soil and before its own partisans."

GLASGOW HERALD
"The success of the Scots was primarily another demonstration that Scottish skill, science and trickery will still prevail."

THE TIMES
"It was not so much defeat that England suffered as humiliation."

SPORTING CHRONICLE
"To the skirl of the bagpipes Scotland caused the rose of England to wither and die at Wembley."

THE BULLETIN & SCOTS PICTORIAL
"Each man was playing to the top of his form, the skill and judgement was a delight to watch."

Provincial papers were equally as rewarding. The *Dumfries and Galloway Standard* noted, "The work of the Scottish side was as near perfection as any team is ever likely to attain, and from the very start the English side were in difficulties." The respected *Athletic News*, the weekly sporting paper widely read in those days before mass radio and TV media, went to great lengths to debate Scotland's marvellous performance. Their correspondent, Ivan Sharpe, wrote that England were "bewildered, run to a standstill, made to appear utterly inferior footballers, by a team whose play was as cultured and beautiful as I ever expect to see". The former England amateur player went on, "sensation it was; no other word adequately describes the utter humiliation of the English XI who were made to look schoolboyish in the second-half and were chasing the ball so that in very truth, there were times when they could not get a kick of it."

The reasons for victory were several. The drenched Wembley turf undoubtedly gave Scotland an advantage with their highly skilled ball players able to run to a defender who always risked a tumble if he attempted a challenge. Ted Hufton, England's 'keeper, said, "It gave them the perfect footing for their skill." Scotland also had the touch of Dame Fortune every great side needs. Hughie Gallacher noted, "Those few early seconds really decided which way the game would go. If Smith had scored with that cross-shot of his, England might have gone on to pile up a big score." Alex James said the team's secret was "the audacious confidence of Jackson and the determination of Hughie Gallacher that gave us the inspiration we needed." Scotland had everything that day . . . team work, ball control, positional play, finishing. Even the necessary yard was allowed for the skidding ball.

Scottish selectors deserve praise too. They had had the courage to bank on skill, and for once it worked for them. Scotland's forwards reached dazzling heights; Jackson and Morton on the wings in particular tormented Jones and Goodall all afternoon and the more subdued Dunn was a workhorse. Above all, the flamboyant musketeers of Jackson, James and Gallacher were a treat to watch, each complementary to the other. While the star names took the headlines the planning for the success was the half-back line. Gibson, Bradshaw and especially McMullan were masters of the game and exercised a controlling influence on the contest. McMullan was to say that England made it easy for them, the home half-backs had been helping their own full-backs cope with Jackson and Morton due to their impact, and this left the midfield totally free with vast open spaces to exploit. Alec Jackson, with his stunning hat-trick, was hailed man-of-the-match by many of the press contingent.

As to England, they were a demoralised lot when the referee's whistle blew time. The last time an English team had conceded five goals was way back in 1882 and they were not to lose by a similar margin until the Hungarians visited Wembley in 1953. They finished bottom of the Home International Championship without a point to their name and had lost all three games for the first time. It had been the worst season in the country's history. The media, while analysing England's failings,

DAZZLING SCOTS DISPLAY

Football That Delighted 80,000 Crowd at Wembley

ENGLAND BEATEN AT ALL POINTS

The Scots team surprised even its sponsors on Saturday. They defeated England in the 52nd International between the two countries at Wembley by five goals to one, a margin never dreamt of in view of what had happened in the previous nationals this season.

Brilliant football earned all the Scottish scores, and before the game was half over they had asserted a superiority over the Saxons that simply meant each man was playing at the top of his form. Against the sometimes stern, and certainly never relaxed, opposition of the Englishmen the skill and judgment of the Scots was a delight to watch. The Southern side never struck a similar game, their defence and half-backs being overworked.

A record crowd for any International in London attended the match. The total number who paid was 80,682, and distinguished visitors present included the Duke of York and the King of Afghanistan.

JACKSON AND JAMES THE HEROES

BY "THE BULLETIN'S" SPECIAL CORRESPONDENTS

Never probably in football history has any team retired with greater sense of the feeling that "our duty has been done" than the Scots who hurried off Wembley field on Saturday.

And our duty and pleasure is to pay tribute to those who represented the Thistle.

Rather singular that with so much ado about the 1900 team that the 1928 side should eclipse them. Granted that everything else was equal, was the score not higher by one? It might have been more, and was the match led in England this time, "far frae hame"? We had been told of R. S. M'Coll's

colleagues that probably we should never gaze on their like again! Well, wonders will never cease. And nobody enjoyed the whole totalities better than the boys of the old brigade.

One we knew who was present roared with delight at the antics of James, chuckled with glee at the joyous swing of the Jackson methods, and revelled in the tic-tac thrust, while the Morton delivery "falling upon the earth beneath" at the Hutton goal area nearly sent him daft.

Scots' Grip

But it was good to be Scottish on a day like that. At the end of a perfect day for, as an Englishman granted it's the pleasure, "it had been so great."

Of course not, England were never permitted to make their game. And the longer it lasted the further they revealed.

Little Bits of Luck

Under ordinary circumstances ground and weather conditions might have been said to favour Scotland.

And the Response

No wonder the winger screamed and no surprise that the spectators went wild.

SATURDAY'S FOOTBALL RESULTS AT A GLANCE

SCOTTISH LEAGUE—First Division		
Rangers	3	Clyde	1
Celtic	3	Falkirk	0
Motherwell	3	Partick Thistle	1

INTERNATIONAL		
England	1	Scotland	5
At Wembley.		

ENGLISH LEAGUE—First Division

TO VICTORY!

M'Zellen, Scotland's captain, sending on to Wembley on Saturday. He led his team on to a field of victory for Scotland.

Match report and headlines from The Bulletin, Monday, 2 April 1928.

praised the Scots' display as the main reason for defeat rather than a lack of England performance. England might have performed poorly but with the Scots playing so well it hardly mattered about the opposition. Comparison between the two sides was extreme.

The *Daily Mail* made the comment, "The selectors could not find an English team good enough to stop this very perfect Scottish machine." Their journalist, J.H. Freeman, continued, "The inferiority of the English side was so marked that the confusion and bewilderment of the individual players, against the science and skill and pace of Scotland's dazzling team became positively ludicrous."

Dixie Dean, the man Scottish fans feared most before the kick-off, seldom received the ball in the right places and Bradshaw had the best of the contest. Wingers Hulme and Smith were never allowed any room while Bradford and Kelly, although getting through a heap of hard graft, never hoped to master midfield when their wing-half colleagues Healless and Edwards were snuffed out of the game.

In defence, England's problem lay with all three players in front of goalkeeper Hufton, who put on an admirable performance to keep the score down. Centre-half Tom Wilson, at his best in the air, found the ball on the greasy floor most of the game and, with Gallacher too elusive, was run ragged. Even when the ball was crossed into the goalmouth Scotland's centre-forward had taken the big pivot out of the action with intelligent positioning to allow space in the box for Jackson to exploit. Three of Scotland's goals came this way.

Full-backs Jones and Goodall had afternoons to forget. The *Topical Times* report noted that Jones found Jackson on top form and "could make little of the fast and elusive Scot", while Goodall, "had a rather unfortunate time". To be blunt both received a roasting from Scotland's duo.

The English press made much of the excuse that six men in England's line-up perhaps had a forthcoming FA Cup final on their minds. But the excuse was a feeble one. The England versus Scotland encounter was just as important a fixture then, and, of course, Alec Jackson had no psychological problems in the Scots side. There was no excuse. England had been well and truly thrashed.

The Bulletin noted, "It was good to be Scottish on a day like that," and so it was. Beaming faces and a glow of satisfaction were evident from the Scots contingent. The thousands of Caledonian fans revelled in one long, wild and well-behaved party that lasted from 4.40 p.m. on Saturday into the early hours of Sunday morning. The pubs and clubs of London's West End were a throng of singing Scots and London welcomed them, unlike more recent visits. Scotland's performance and the dedication of their followers had captured the imagination of the Londoners. The *Glasgow*

The match ball preserved and inscribed.

Herald related that fans were "cheered and praised, and in the big popular restaurants and hotel lounges bands rendered programmes of popular Scottish songs". The *Glasgow Evening Times* reporter noted, "Everybody wanted to make a fuss over us." They sang their way back to the railway stations, echoing into the night sky, in seemingly never-ending groups. A new song rang out specially for the occasion to the tune of *John Brown's Body* – "We'll crown Alec Jackson King of Scotland." At Euston there was dancing on the platform to an improvised jazz band mixed oddly with the pipes.

With so many travelling fans there was, remarkably, only one incident of note, even more surprising considering the amount of alcohol that must have been consumed. A certain David Baird of Craigneuk fell on to the railway lines while waiting for a train and had to spend the night in hospital. Still, it happened after the game so he probably didn't care too much!

The Wembley Wizards achieved what every Scot longs for, the annihilation of the English. With the resounding victory the biennial

Alec Jackson, hat-trick hero for Scotland at Wembley and man-of-the-match.

trek to Wembley was also born. As soon as fans had returned to their home stations scattered over Scotland they started to save for the next journey south and to plan the next display of national patriotism. It is a journey which continues with fervour to this day.

Of course Scotland were not always to produce such a majestic show at Wembley. In fact they have never approached the performance since, one of the reasons why the Wizards' display has grown in stature over the years until it has become folklore. England held the advantage up to the Second World War, including a 5-2 victory when Scotland next ventured to Wembley, in 1930. On that day the Scots were termed 'Wembley Follies' rather than Wembley Wizards. It was not until 1967, almost 40 years later, that the Wizards' performance was remotely approached – the day that England, as World Cup-holders, fell to Bremner, Baxter and the rest of Bobby Brown's team. Apart from 1928, Scotland have never scored more than three goals at Wembley and have only won eight games there in 28 fixtures played. Only once since 1882 have Scotland scored five goals in a full international against England home or away, that in 1928.

The Wembley Wizards have been praised many times over. Kevin McCarra wrote, in his *Pictorial History of Scottish Football*, that the game is "one of the principal glories in the history of our sport". The match and those 11 immortals who took part will be written and talked about for generations to come. One old-time professional who watched the game said they "opened my eyes to real football, showed me how it should be played".

It was the showpiece of Scottish football, the day when five all-time-greats – James, McMullan, Gallacher, Morton and Jackson – linked together in beautiful perfection. Saturday, 31 March 1928 has gone down in history as the "Day of the Wizards", and as *Athletic News* reported, "All Scotland should have been there to see it."

MATCH STATISTICS

Date: Saturday, 31 March 1928

Venue: Empire Stadium, Wembley

England: Hufton (West Ham), Goodall (captain, Huddersfield Town), Jones (Blackburn Rvs), Edwards (Leeds Utd), Wilson (Huddersfield Town), Healless (Blackburn Rvs), Hulme (Arsenal), Kelly (Huddersfield Town), Dean (Everton), Bradford (Birmingham City), Smith (Huddersfield Town).

Scotland: Harkness (Queen's Park), Nelson (Cardiff City), Law (Chelsea), Gibson (Aston Villa), Bradshaw (Bury), McMullan (captain, Manchester City), Jackson (Huddersfield Town), Dunn (Hibernian), Gallacher (Newcastle Utd), James (Preston), Morton (Rangers)

Referee: W. Bell (Scotland)

Linesmen: J.L. Morrison (Scotland), S.F. Rous (England)

Result: Scotland 5 (2)   England 1 (0)

Goals: *Scotland* – Jackson (3 mins), James (44 mins), Jackson (65 mins), James (66 mins), Jackson (85 mins)
England – Kelly (89 mins)

Attendance: 80,682

FACTS AND FIGURES

Scotland versus England
Full internationals at Wembley Stadium

12 April	1924	Draw	1-1
31 March	1928	Scotland	5-1
5 April	1930	England	5-2
9 April	1932	England	3-0
14 April	1934	England	3-0
4 April	1936	Draw	1-1
9 April	1938	Scotland	1-0
12 April	1947	Draw	1-1
9 April	1949	Scotland	3-1
14 April	1951	Scotland	3-2
18 April	1953	Draw	2-2
2 April	1955	England	7-2
6 April	1957	England	2-1
11 April	1959	England	1-0
15 April	1961	England	9-3
6 April	1963	Scotland	2-1
10 April	1965	Draw	2-2
15 April	1967	Scotland	3-2
10 May	1969	England	4-1
22 May	1971	England	3-1
19 May	1973	England	1-0
24 May	1975	England	5-1
4 June	1977	Scotland	2-1
26 May	1979	England	3-1
23 May	1981	Scotland	1-0
1 June	1983	England	2-0
23 April	1986	England	2-1
21 May	1988	England	1-0

Wartime internationals at Wembley Stadium

4 October	1941	England	2-0
17 January	1942	England	3-0
10 October	1942	Draw	0-0
19 February	1944	England	6-2
14 October	1944	England	6-2

Overall record at Wembley 1924-1988
Played *28* Scotland won *8* England won *15* Drawn *5* Scotland *40* England *66*
including wartime
Played *33* Scotland won *8* England won *19* Drawn *6* Scotland *44* England *83*

Largest Scottish victory at Wembley
5-1 in 1928
3-1 in 1949

Largest English victory at Wembley
9-3 in 1961
7-2 in 1955
5-1 in 1975

Four or more Scottish goals at Wembley
Once only; 5-1 in 1928

Hat-trick by a Scotland player at Wembley
Once only; Alec Jackson in 1928

Hat-trick by an English player at Wembley
On two occasions; D. Wilshaw (4) in 1955, J. Greaves in 1961

Hat-trick by a Scotland player in any full England international
On six occasions; J. McDougall (1878), G. Ker (1880), J. Smith (1881 & 1883), R.S. McColl (1900) and Alec Jackson (1928)

Scotland versus England

Overall record in full internationals 1872-1989
In Scotland
Played *54* Scotland won *23* England won *18* Drawn *13* Scotland *81* England *73*

In England
Played *53* Scotland won *17* England won *25* Drawn *11* Scotland *87* England *115*

Total
Played *107* Scotland won *40* England won *43* Drawn *24* Scotland *168* England *188*

Largest Scottish victory
7-2 in 1878
6-1 in 1881

Largest English victory
9-3 in 1961

Scotland v England venues
In Scotland
Hamilton Crescent, First Hampden, Cathkin Park, Second Hampden, Ibrox Park, Parkhead, Hampden Park

In England
Kennington Oval, Bramall Lane, Ewood Park, Richmond, Goodison Park, Crystal Palace, Villa Park, St James Park, Stamford Bridge, Old Trafford, Wembley Stadium

Highest attendance
In Scotland
149,547 at Hampden Park in 1937

In England
100,000 at Wembley in 1979

BIBLIOGRAPHY

BOOKS

Allison, W. – *Rangers, The New Era*
Archer, I. – *The Jags* (History of Partick Thistle)
Binns, G.S. – *Huddersfield Town 75 Years On*
Buchan, C. – *Lifetime in Football*
Bury FC – *Bury 1885-1985*
Busby, M. – *My Story*
Cheshire, S. & Hockings, R. – *Chelsea FC*
Clareborough, D. – *Sheffield United, the First 100 Years*
Crampsey, R. – *The Scots Footballer*
Crampsey, R. – *The Game for Game's Sake* (History of Queen's Park)
Crooks, J. – *The Bluebirds* (A Who's Who of Cardiff City)
Docherty/Thomson – *100 Years of Hibs*
Dykes, G. – *Oldham Athletic: A Complete Record.*
Farnsworth, R. – *Wednesday (History of Sheffield Wednesday)*
Finn, R.L. – *A History of Chelsea*
Gibson/Pickles – *Association Football & The Men Who Made It*
Goble, R. – *Manchester City: A Complete Record*
Goodyear, D. & Matthews, T. – *Aston Villa: A Complete Record*
Halliday, S. – *Rangers*
Hamlyn – *Hamlyn Book of Soccer Records*
Harding, J. – *Alex James, Life of a Football Legend*
Heart of Midlothian FC – *A Pictorial History*
Inglis, S. – *The Football Grounds of England & Wales*
Jackson, P. – *The Cardiff City Story*
James, A. & Woods, L. – *The Official History of Preston NE*
James, B. – *England v Scotland*
Jenkins, D. & Stennett C. – *Wembley 1927*
Joannou, P. – *Newcastle United: A Complete Record*
Joannou, P. – *The Hughie Gallacher Story*
Joy, B. – *Forward Arsenal*
Kelly, S.F. – *Back Page Football*
Lamming, D. & Farrer, M. – *A Century of English International Football*
Lamming, D. – *A Scottish Soccer International Who's Who*
Lamming, D. – *A Who's Who of Liverpool*
Litster, J. – *Raith Rovers, A Centenary History*
Longman – *Longman's Chronicle of the 20th Century*
McCarra, K. & Keevans, H. – *100 Cups*

McCarra, K. – *Scottish Football, A Pictorial History*
McGlone, D. & McLure, W. – *The Juniors: 100 Years*
MacKay, J.R. – *The Hibees*
Mackie, A. – *The Hearts*
McPhail, R. & Herron, A. – *Legend*
Matthews, T. – *Wolves*
Morris, P. – *Aston Villa*
Pawson, T. – *100 Years of the FA Cup*
Pead, B. – *Liverpool: A Complete Record*
Rafferty, J. – *100 Years of Scottish Football*
Rickaby, J. – *Aberdeen: A Complete Record*
Rippon, A. – *England!*
Rippon, A. & Ward, A. – *Derby County: A Complete Record*
Roberts, J. – *Everton*
Robertson, H.C. – *The New Scottish Football Fact Book*
Ross, I. & Smailes, G. – *Everton: A Complete Record*
Sharpe, I. – *40 Years in Football*
Soar, P. & Tyler, M. – *Arsenal Centenary History*
Taylor, H. – *Great Masters of Scottish Football*
Walsh, N. – *Dixie Dean*
Ward, A. – *The Manchester City Story*
Ward, A. – *Scotland: The Team*
Webster, J. – *The Dons*

REPORTS, PROGRAMMES, ANNUALS ETC
Athletic News Annuals 1914-1939
Gamage's Annuals 1914-1929
Rothmans Yearbooks 1970-1989
Topical Times Annuals 1921-1929
Association of Football Statisticians: various reports, yearbooks
England v Scotland official programmes 1928-1989
Scottish Football Association: minutes of meetings 1928
Scottish Football Association: accounts 1928
Scottish Football Historian reports: various editions

NEWSPAPERS & MAGAZINES
The Times; The Scotsman; Glasgow Herald; The Bulletin & Scots Pictorial; Dumfries & Galloway Standard; Sunday Chronicle; Daily Mail; Glasgow Evening Times; Athletic News; Daily Mirror; Sporting Chronicle; All Sports Weekly (all for 1928)
Charles Buchan's Football Monthly: various editions
The Footballer: various editions

SPECIFIC ARTICLES
Hughie Gallacher Tells All – Hughie Gallacher, *Newcastle Weekly Chronicle*, 1950
40 Years of Fun & Games – Jack Harkness, *Sunday Post*, 1962
Football . . . with the Lid off! – Alex James, *News of the World*, 1937

THE ENGLAND TEAM

Back Row: *Goodall, Hufton, Jones.*
Middle Row: *Edwards, Wilson, Healless.*
Front Row: *Hulme, Kelly, Dean, Bradford, Smith.*

THE SCOTLAND TEAM

Back Row: *Nelson, Harkness, Law.*
Middle Row: *Gibson, Bradshaw, McMullan.*
Front Row: *Jackson, Dunn, Gallacher, James, Morton.*